Planet & People

Second Edition

Leaving Certificate

Geography

Sue Honan & Sue Mulholland

MENTOR
BOOKS

MENTOR BOOKS
43 Furze Road
Sandyford Industrial Estate
Dublin 18
Tel: 01-2952112
Fax: 01-2952114
Website: www.mentorbooks.ie
Email: admin@mentorbooks.ie

Edited by:	Treasa O'Mahony
Subject Editor:	Dr Tom Hunt
Book Design & Typesetting:	Nicola Sedgwick Kathryn O'Sullivan Mary Byrne
Cover Design:	Mary Byrne
Illustrations:	Michael Phillips

ISBN: 978–1–906623-67-8
© Sue Honan, Sue Mulholland 2011

1 3 5 7 9 10 8 6 4 2

Printed in Ireland by Colourbooks Ltd.

Contents

GEOECOLOGY

Acknowledgements

Brazilian Embassy; Jean Cantwell; Clonakilty Agricultural College; Department of Agriculture; Jean Duffy; Tony Dunne; John Englishby; John and Maureen Enright; examsupport.ie; Dermot McCarthy; Con McGinley; Billy and Mimi McNabb; Anna Marie Margan; Anne Mulligan; Brigid Murray; *NewScientist*; Michael Redmond; Val Redmond; Scientific American; Staff and Students at St Laurence College, Loughlinstown; Staff and students of St Mary's College, Dundalk; State Examinations Commission; S. Sydenham and R. Thomas (Rainforest Biome); Jimmy Weldon; Anita White.

Dedication

For Chris, Eleanor and Maedhbh Honan

For Gerard, Patricia and Eoghan Mulholland

Chapter 1
Soils

At the end of this chapter you should be able to:

- **Describe soil composition.**
- **Explain how soil is formed.**
- **Describe a typical soil profile.**
- **Name and describe the main characteristics of soil.**
- **Name and explain processes that affect soil.**
- **Describe the factors affecting soil formation.**
- **Explain how these factors and processes influence soil characteristics.**

Contents

KEY THEME

Soils develop from the weathering of rocks in situ and from re-deposited weathered material. Soils are affected by their immediate environment and by a combination of processes operating in that environment.

Introduction

All soils form as a result of the action of several factors affecting the earth's surface. These factors are climate, relief, parent material, living things and time. These factors combine to influence the many processes at work in soil formation, e.g. leaching and weathering, which together give each soil its own specific soil characteristics, e.g. soil colour and texture.

1.1 Soil composition

What is soil made of?

Soil is composed of a number of ingredients/constituents.

1. **Mineral matter** – rock particles from the bedrock and weathered rock.
2. **Air** – found in the pore spaces between the rock grains.
3. **Water** – also found in the pore spaces between the rock grains. In dry weather, water forms a thin film around the grains. In wet weather, it fills the pores.
4. **Humus** – a black sticky gel produced from decaying organic matter such as leaves and dead animals.
5. **Living organisms** – earthworms, beetles, fungi, bacteria.

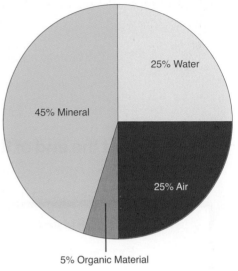

Fig. 1 Composition of soil

The components of soil are mixed in different quantities to create different soil types. Climate, vegetation and time play a role in creating soil. However, climate is the single most important factor in determining what a soil will be like as climate influences vegetation, the rate of weathering and soil-forming processes in an area.

Fig. 2 Bare rock

Fig. 3 Lichen/moss on rock

Fig. 4 Healthy plant growth on soil

Soil formation

Soil is the result of the continuous cycle involving the interaction of climate, rocks and living things.

1 Solid rock particles are broken down by mechanical weathering to form small soil grains. These make up the 'skeleton' of the soil.

2 Chemical weathering releases important nutrients from the rock grains, e.g. phosphorous, potassium, calcium.

3 Seeds are blown or carried onto the soil grains and may grow into plants that enrich the soil when they die. Early plants that can grow in young soils include mosses and lichens.

5 This cycle continues until the soil reaches its maximum fertility given the climate it is in.

4 Micro-organisms decompose the remains of plants and form humus, which further enriches the soil and helps bind the soil grains together. These micro-organisms improve the fertility of the soil, enabling a greater variety of plants to grow.

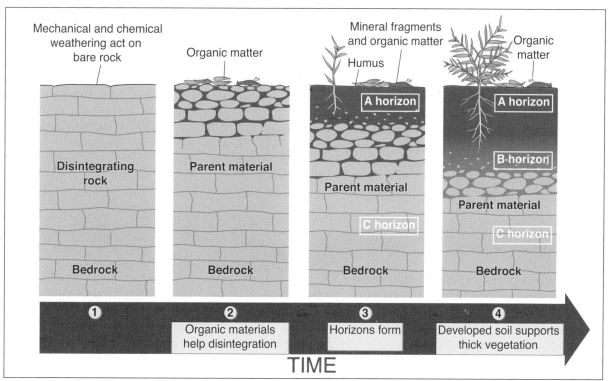

Fig. 5 Soil formation

7

1.2 Soil profiles

A section of soil extending from the surface to the bedrock below is called a **soil profile**.

Fig. 6 Note the clear horizons.

A soil profile may show different layers called **horizons** within the soil.

These layers have been created by a combination of processes, such as the passage of water through the soil and animal activity within the soil.

A general soil profile is shown below:

The O **Organic Horizon** has a high percentage of organic matter, usually greater than 20% to 30%. Leaves, dead plants and dead animals collect on the surface (**litter layer**). This layer is rich in micro-organisms. Humus is formed as the dead organic matter begins to decay.

The **A Horizon** is typically referred to as the topsoil. It is characterised by organic matter mixed with mineral soil grains. It is a dark-coloured horizon. An A horizon may be altered by burrowing animals and the addition of organic material (fertilisers). This horizon has the most root activity and is usually the most productive layer of soil.

The **B Horizon** is also called the subsoil. This is a zone of mineral accumulation where rainwater percolates through the soil and deposits material leached from above.

The **C Horizon** is not affected by the weathering process. The overlying soil horizons and materials often but not always develop from the C horizon.

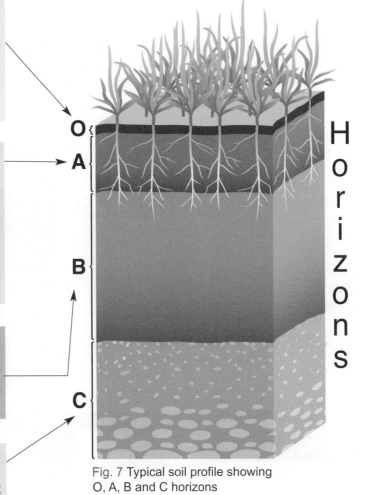

Fig. 7 Typical soil profile showing O, A, B and C horizons

1.3 Soil characteristics

All soils can be described according to their **characteristics**. There are six soil characteristics. These characteristics combine to form different soil types.

1. Colour
2. Structure
3. Texture
4. Humus content
5. Acidity/alkalinity of the soil (soil pH)
6. Water content/retention

Characteristic 1: Colour

➤ Soils have a range of colours. Peat is dark black, other soils may be bright red or yellow. The colour of a soil depends on factors such as the rock it developed upon (**parent material**) and the **processes** that have occurred such as leaching (see page 15). For example, if the parent material is sandstone, the soils that develop on it may be pale brown. Soils affected by leaching may also be pale in colour.

➤ Soil colour affects the temperature of the soil. Dark-coloured soils warm up more quickly and this may increase the activity of the living things in the soil and so encourage humus production. Pale-coloured soils reflect more sunlight and are slower to warm up.

Characteristic 2: Structure

➤ Soil structure is a description of the way in which soil grains are stuck together by humus and clay particles. If you pull a plant from the ground, its roots will hold soil grains. Look closely and you will see that the grains are in small lumps which are called **peds**. The shape of these peds indicates the structure of the soil.

➤ The **pore spaces** between the peds hold air and water and are important for plants to access air and water in the soil. Overcropping and overgrazing damage the structure of the soil, reducing its ability to support plant growth.

Some common soil structures:
1. Crumb/granular
2. Blocky
3. Platy

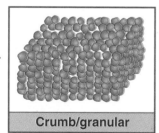
Crumb/granular

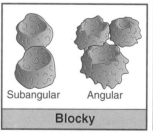
Subangular   Angular
Blocky

Platy

Fig. 8 Three common ped shapes

Crumb/granular structure

In this structure the peds are small rounded clumps of soil particles similar to breadcrumbs in size. This type of structure is very good for holding air and water. It is well drained and plants grow well in it. Loam soils have this structure.

Fig. 9 Crumb/granular structure

Fig. 10 Clay soil

Blocky structure

In this structure the peds are closely packed angular blocks. It is well drained but can be compacted easily and plants have difficulty growing in it when this occurs. Sandy soils have this structure. The addition of humus to the soil can improve this structure for plant growth.

Platy structure

In this structure the soil peds are arranged in thin layers. It forms in clay soils and prevents good drainage of water through the soil. Plants have difficulty growing in soils with this structure.

Characteristic 3: Texture

Texture describes how a soil feels to the touch. The texture of a soil is controlled by the amount of sand, silt and clay particles in it. Different soils textures have different amounts of pore space, which affects the amount of water (its water content) and air in the soil. The texture of the soil can also affect its soil structure. Clay soils have a platy structure and loam soils have a crumb structure. There are four main textures:

(a) clay **(b)** sandy **(c)** silty **(d)** loam

When describing soil textures, the terms **silt**, **sand** and **clay** are important because they indicate the particular **size of the mineral grains** in a soil.

Type of soil	Description
Clay	Particle diameter is less than 0.002 mm. **Not visible to the naked eye.**
Silt	Particle diameter is between 0.002 mm and 0.05 mm. Barely visible to the naked eye.
Sand	Particle diameter is between 0.05 mm and 2 mm. Visible to the naked eye.

Fig. 11 Description of soil grains

Clay soils

➤ Clay soils contain 40-100% clay.
➤ Clay soil contains the smallest-sized particles.
➤ Clay particles form a sticky soil when wet and will generally hold a shape after drying.
➤ Clay soil is naturally high in nutrients so plants grow well.
➤ In summer, it is often baked dry with visible surface cracks, making it difficult to get water to the roots of plants. In winter, it can be constantly wet and waterlogging is common. At most times of the year, it is difficult to dig.
➤ If a soil feels sticky and smooth and it holds together like playdough, it is probably a clay soil.

Fig. 12 Clay soil is used to make clay pots.

Silty soils

➤ Silty soils contain 40-100% silt.

➤ Silty soil contains particles that are smaller than sand particles but larger than clay particles.

➤ Silt feels powdery when rubbed between your thumb and forefinger.

➤ Silty soil peds stick together when wet, but they will not hold their shape after they dry.

➤ Silty soils can be badly drained but do not often become waterlogged.

Fig. 13 Silty soils

Sandy soils

➤ Sandy soils contain 85-100% sand.

➤ Sandy soil contains particles that can be seen with the naked eye and feels gritty when rubbed between your thumb and forefinger. Sandy soils tend not to stick together when wet.

➤ Waterlogging is rare in sandy soils as they are very free-draining. However, watering and feeding of plants is needed on a regular basis because the nutrients drain away easily.

➤ Sandy soil is quick to warm up in the spring, so sowing and planting can be done earlier in the year than in clay or silty soil.

Fig. 14 Sandy soils

Loam soils

➤ Loam soils contain roughly equal amounts of clay, sand and silt.

➤ Most plants will grow in loam soils.

➤ It is brown and feels crumbly in texture and similar to that found in well maintained gardens.

➤ This soil is rarely waterlogged in winter or dry in summer and supports a wide range of plants.

➤ Loamy soil is light and easy to dig and is naturally high in nutrients.

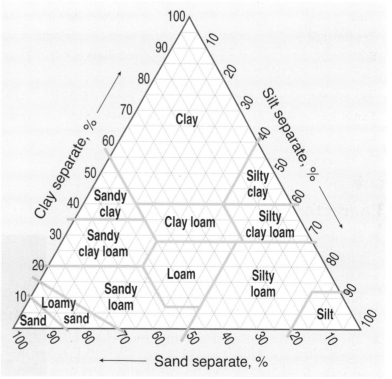

Fig. 15 Soil textures

Appearance of soil under lens	Feel of soil between fingers		Rolling of soil between fingers	Textures of soil
	Dry	Wet		
Large (sandy) grains absent or very few in amount	Smooth and non-grainy Slightly gritty	Generally very sticky Plastic/pliable	Gives long threads which bend into rings, similar to the effect of rolling a strand of playdough between fingers	Clay Sandy clay
Many sand grains present	Slightly gritty	Moderately plastic /pliable	Gives threads with difficulty which will NOT easily bend into rings	Clay loam Silty clay loam Sandy clay loam
Sand grains present but silt and clay predominating	Smooth	Smooth	Forms threads with broken appearance	Silty loam
Comparable proportions of sand, silt and clay	Gritty	Slightly plastic/pliable	Gives threads with great difficulty	Loam
Sand grains predominate	Gritty	Not plastic or pliable – only slight cohesion	Gives threads with very great difficulty	Sandy loam
Mostly sand	Very gritty	Forms a flowing mass	Does not give threads	Loamy sand Sand

Fig. 16 Tests to determine soil texture

Characteristic 4: Humus content

➤ Humus is a dark black gel formed from rotting plant and vegetable material in a soil.

➤ Micro-organisms such as fungi and bacteria add humus by decomposing dead material.

➤ Humus helps to bind soil grains together.

➤ The humus content of soil is important due to its ability to support plant growth. As it is washed into the ground by rain, humus adds nutrients to the soil (see Fig. 19). Living things in the soil also add humus to the soil with their droppings. In addition, earthworms, beetles and insect larvae

Fig. 17 Fungi decompose dead leaves into humus.

burrow through the soil. When these creatures die, their bodies decompose adding more humus to the soil.

➤ Humus content affects the colour, texture and structure of soils. Soils rich in humus tend to be dark, with a good crumb structure and loam texture.

➤ Humus increases the ability of the soil to hold water.

➤ The addition of natural and artificial fertilisers adds to humus content of soils.

Fig. 18 Natural fertiliser adds humus to soil.

Nutrient	What it does in the plant
Iron	Used by plants to make chlorophyll, important for photosynthesis
Calcium	Used in plant cell walls and in starch production, e.g. potatoes
Nitrogen	Used to make plant proteins, carbohydrate and cells
Potassium	Important for plant growth. Regulates opening and closing of pores (stomata) in leaves, essential for photosynthesis and water transport.

Fig. 19 Some important plant nutrients and their function

Characteristic 5: Acidity/alkalinity of the soil (soil pH)

➤ The pH of a soil is a measure of how acidic or alkaline it is. The acidity/alkalinity levels control which plants and animals will live in the soil.

➤ The pH of a soil is affected by the rock it developed upon (parent material). Acidic soils develop on acidic rocks such as granite while alkaline soils develop on alkaline rocks such as limestone.

➤ Most plants prefer a slightly acidic soil with a pH of 6.5. Peat soils are extremely acidic and contain few living things within them.

➤ Neutral soils are most suitable for bacteria which help to release nutrients such as nitrogen into the soil.

➤ Very acidic soils lack calcium and potassium and this stunts plant growth.

➤ Acidic soil also discourages the presence of living things which reduces the humus content of soils.

➤ A fertile agricultural soil has a pH of 6.5.

Characteristic 6: Water content/retention

Water is important for a soil for the following reasons:

- It enables plants to absorb nutrients dissolved from the mineral grains.
- It enables the survival of micro-organisms responsible for humus formation.
- It reduces soil erosion by the wind.
- It enables the formation of soil horizons.
- It binds soil particles together.

The amount of water a soil can hold depends on the humus content, texture and structure. Soils rich in humus can hold more moisture than those which lack humus.

Soils that have a sandy texture are often dry because water drains through the large pore spaces between the sand grains very quickly. A clay soil tends to hold more water due to the very small

grains which have a large surface area and therefore hold more water around them.

Soils with a platy structure tend to become waterlogged as water cannot easily pass through this type of structure and gathers between the layers of the platy peds.

1.4 Processes affecting soil characteristics

No two soils are alike in their characteristics (e.g. colour, texture). In order to explain these differences, we must examine the **processes** that occur within a soil and then the overriding environmental factors that control these processes.

The eight major processes affecting soil characteristics are:

1. Weathering
2. Humification
3. Leaching
4. Podzolisation
5. Gleying
6. Laterisation
7. Salinisation
8. Calcification

The factors of climate, relief, rock type, living things and time all influence which of these processes occur in a region. These in turn influence the different soil characteristics.

The overall effect of the above processes is to form layers/ horizons in a soil profile. These processes also affect soil characteristics such as colour, texture, mineral content, humus content, soil pH and water content.

Process 1: Weathering

➤ Weathering is the **physical and chemical breakdown of rocks into smaller pieces** and is responsible for providing the mineral part of the soil.

➤ Soil grains can be released from rocks by mechanical weathering such as freeze–thaw action and by chemical weathering.

➤ The soil grains produced by weathering keep the characteristics of the parent rock such as pH, texture and colour. For example if the mineral grains have come from weathered sandstone they will be acidic, pale brown and sandy in texture. If the mineral grains have come from the weathering of shale, they will be black, platy structured and clay in texture. If the rock grains have come from limestone, the soil will be alkaline.

➤ Chemical weathering processes such as carbonation and oxidation can release nutrients such as phosphorous, calcium and iron from the mineral grains. The chemical weathering of limestone by carbonation leads to dark brown alkaline soils rich in calcium. The process of hydrolysis is responsible for releasing clay particles from granite rocks and the process of oxidation releases iron.

Fig. 20 These pieces of scree are being mechanically weathered into soil.

Process 2: Humification

➤ Humification is the method by which **dead organic matter is converted into humus** by the action of fungi and bacteria. Humification is important for soil as it makes it fertile.

➤ Humification releases nutrients into the soil.

➤ Rain washes the humus into the soil where it is used by plant roots as a nutrient.

➤ Climate is an important factor affecting the rate of humification.

➤ In hot humid climates such as a tropical climate, humification is very fast.

➤ In deserts, the lack of water may limit the amount of humus that is washed into the soil. The dry conditions do not favour the growth of fungi or the activity of bacteria which reduces the amount of humus produced.

➤ In temperate regions such as Ireland, humification occurs more slowly in winter.

➤ In cold arctic climates, humification may stop completely and dead plant and animal material will not decompose at all or extremely slowly (e.g. ice age woolly mammoths preserved in Siberian permafrost).

Fig. 21 Fungi decompose a dead branch into humus.

Process 3: Leaching

➤ Leaching is the **removal of nutrients from the soil by water**.

➤ Rainwater washes soluble substances down through the pores in the soil. In very wet conditions, nutrients are washed from the soil altogether. In drier regions, minerals build up in a layer lower down in the soil.

➤ A certain amount of leaching is needed to wash humus into soil. However, excessive leaching is bad for soil because it makes it infertile.

➤ In general the A and B horizons may lack minerals due to leaching and appear pale in colour.

Process 4: Podzolisation

➤ This is a type of **leaching that occurs where rainwater is more acidic**.

➤ **Podzol soils** form under coniferous forests. As these forests die and decompose, they add to the acidity of the rainwater. The water seeping through the soil beneath this dead vegetation becomes acidic due to the absorption of humic acids from rotting vegetation.

➤ The acidic rainwater dissolves all soil minerals except quartz. Quartz is a very resistant mineral. The top layer of podzolised soils is ash grey in colour due to the presence of quartz crystals. The layer below is enriched with the dissolved minerals from above and is darker in appearance.

➤ Podzols may also contain a layer of reddish iron oxide (rust) in the B horizon. This is formed when the iron-rich minerals collect together and is called a **hard pan** or **iron pan** and can prevent water from draining through the soil.

Fig. 22 Podzol soils form under coniferous forests.

Process 5: Gleying

➤ Gleying is the process by which the **soil is waterlogged and lacks oxygen**.

➤ In a gley soil the pores between the soil peds are filled with water for all or part of the year. This prevents living things in the soil receiving oxygen. They lack organic matter as little can grow in such wet, oxygen-poor (**anaerobic**) conditions.

➤ Climate and relief can lead to the gleying process occurring. Heavy rainfall can lead to soils being waterlogged. If the land has dips and hollows which prevent

Fig. 23 Waterlogged gley soil

the drainage of water from the land, water can collect in the hollows and the soils around them are gleyed.

➤ Due to the lack of oxygen, gley soils have patches of blue/grey colouration.

➤ They are common in Ireland's drumlin belt (County Cavan, County Monaghan) and where the bedrock is impermeable (shale regions of County Clare).

Process 6: Laterisation

➤ This is a type of **severe chemical weathering**.

➤ It occurs in tropical and equatorial regions of the world where leaching, carbonation and high temperatures combine to dissolve all minerals out of the soil except iron and aluminium oxides.

➤ In areas of heavy rainfall such as the tropics and equatorial regions, all alkaline material is removed from the soil by the chemical weathering process of **carbonation**. The pH of the soil is slightly acidic.

➤ The oxidation of iron and aluminium gives the soils a red appearance and they are known as latosols. If the soil dries out, it turns into a hard laterite.

Fig. 25 A boy breaking latosols into bricks

Fig. 24 Laterite bricks

Process 7: Salinisation

➤ Salinisation occurs when **mineral salts move up through the soil** towards the surface instead of down into the soil.

➤ This process can happen in hot desert areas of the world where precipitation is low. In these climatic conditions the amount of water evaporating out of the soil is greater than precipitation falling onto it.

➤ Evaporation causes salts in ground water to rise through the soil and collect in the upper layers. Salt is deposited on the surface as a hard white crust. If the salt concentration becomes too high, plants are poisoned and die.

Fig. 26 Salinised soil in Death Valley, USA

➤ Salinisation is a problem for farmers who have to wash the salt crust away or break it up before their crops can grow.

➤ Irrigation salinisation is caused by excess water from irrigation which raises the water table, bringing salt to the surface. Irrigation salinisation can be reduced by using less water on crops and by growing crops which require less irrigation. Irrigation salinisation in Australia is estimated to cost the farming community €307 million each year.

Process 8: Calcification

➤ This is the process by which **calcium carbonate is concentrated near the surface** of the soil in a process similar to salinisation.

➤ Calcification occurs in regions of low rainfall, such as in the interiors of continents, e.g. the prairies of North America and the steppes of Russia.

➤ The amount of water drawn up through the soil by plants (**transpiration**) may be greater than the precipitation falling on the soil. As a result of this, calcium

Fig. 27 Fertile calcified soil

carbonate builds up in the upper layer (A Horizon) of the soil.

➤ Calcium carbonate is a very useful substance for plants and these soils often have lush grass growth. When the grass dies, calcium carbonate is returned to the soil.

➤ Calcified soils are often alkaline in pH.

Summary of soil-forming processes

Soil-forming process	Where it occurs	What it does	Soils affected
Weathering: Chemical and Mechanical	Everywhere. Some areas may have more chemical weathering, e.g. hot wet tropical climates. Other regions have more mechanical weathering, e.g. arctic regions.	Mechanical weathering provides the mineral portion of a soil. Chemical weathering provides important elements to soil, e.g. calcium.	All soils
Humification	Cool temperate oceanic climate. Deciduous forest regions, e.g. Ireland	Fungi and bacteria decompose dead matter to form humus. This is washed into soil by rain.	Brown earth soils
Leaching	Any wet climatic region. Does not occur very much in deserts or arctic regions.	Rainwater washes nutrients down into the soil from the O horizon.	All soils where rain occurs
Podzolisation	Temperate climates under coniferous forest, e.g. Ireland.	Leaching by acidic rainwater. Minerals are dissolved from soil and washed down. This makes the B horizon pale coloured. Minerals then collect in the soil as crusty rusty-coloured hard pan.	Podzol
Gleying	Wet areas and poorly drained regions such as hollows and lake edges, e.g. drumlin belt of Monaghan.	Soil is waterlogged. Prevents the action of bacteria and fungi in the soil. Soil is patchy blue/grey coloured.	Gley soils
Laterisation	Equatorial and tropical climates	Extreme chemical weathering and leaching removes all minerals from a soil except aluminium and iron. Makes soil red/orange.	Latosol
Salinisation	Dry climates such as the Mediterranean and desert climate.	'Reverse leaching'. In dry areas water is drawn up through the soil pores by evaporation. Economic problem in irrigated areas of Australia, California and Spain. Salt is deposited on the soil surface as a white crust. Prevents plants from growing.	Aridisols
Calcification	Interiors of continents such as the prairies of the USA and the steppes of Russia.	Calcium carbonate gathers on the top of the soil due to the action of plants drawing water up from the ground. Rainfall is not sufficient to wash it back down again.	Chernozem

1.5 Factors affecting soil processes and soil characteristics

Climate, relief, parent material, living things and time are important in controlling the formation of soils. They do this by influencing the processes affecting soil (pages 14-17) and soil characteristics (pages 9-14).

Factors affecting soil formation:
1. Climate
2. Relief
3. Parent material
4. Living things
5. Time

Factor 1: Climate

Climate is the single most important factor in soil formation.

➤ This is because climate determines the rate and type of weathering, which soil-forming processes will operate and how much biological activity can occur in the soil.

➤ Soils that have developed in response to particular climatic conditions are called **zonal soils**.

➤ Zonal soils are found in particular climatic regions, e.g. the soil associated with the cool temperate oceanic climate of Ireland is the **brown earth** soil.

➤ Within the world's climatic zones there are variations in relief which cause local climates (micro climates) to occur making it wetter, drier, cooler or warmer than usual. These micro climates may influence the zonal soil, changing it in some way. These altered soils are called **intrazonal** soils, e.g. the gley soils of the drumlin belt in Ireland. Soils that are too young to have developed into full zonal soils are called **azonal soils**.

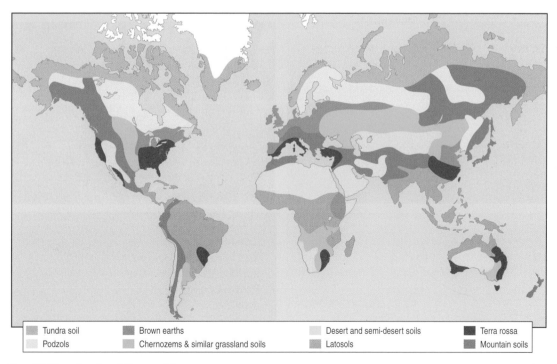

| Tundra soil | Brown earths | Desert and semi-desert soils | Terra rossa |
| Podzols | Chernozems & similar grassland soils | Latosols | Mountain soils |

Fig. 28 Zonal soils of the world

19

Climatic zone	Vegetation	Zonal soil
Tundra	Tundra	Arctic brown soil
Boreal	Coniferous forest (taiga)	Podzol
Cool temperate oceanic	Mixed deciduous forest	Brown earths
Mediterranean	Mediterranean	Red brown soils
Continental	Steppe/prairie	Chernozems
Tropical/ equatorial	Rainforest	Latosols
Desert	Desert	Aridisols

Fig. 29 Zonal soils of the world

Climate influences which soil processes are dominant in an area.

➤ Soils in wet climates can be leached, gleyed or podzolised. In drier areas the soils may be salinised or calcified. Humification and laterisation are dominant in hot humid areas. In colder regions such as the Tundra, the surface may be frozen for most of the year. Biological activity is slowed down and humification is delayed. Thin infertile soils may occur in these regions.

➤ In hot wet climates, such as in the tropical and equatorial zones, chemical weathering is rapid. As a result, deep soils develop.

Climate controls the speed and type of weathering that takes place.

➤ By influencing the type of weathering that occurs in a region, climate can control soil characteristics such as colour, texture, structure, pH and water content.

➤ For example, in hot wet climates, chemical weathering is rapid and wet; acidic soils may occur that are red/orange in colour.

➤ In colder climates mechanical weathering such as freeze-thaw action produces angular stones (scree) which are further weathered into smaller grains that may give the soil a sandy texture.

Fig. 30 Climate is the most important factor affecting the development of soils and therefore the plants and animals that can exist in a region.

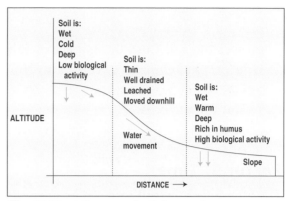

Factor 2: Relief

Relief can influence the depth and drainage of a soil.

➤ In general, sloping land is well drained and soils are quite dry. However, mass movement such as soil creep can occur so soils that develop on slopes are usually quite thin.

➤ Flat upland areas are usually cold and wet. These conditions cause waterlogging and gley soils. Because temperatures are low, the biological activity of animals and micro-organisms is slowed down so dead organic matter builds up but is not converted into humus. Peat is an example of this. As a result, upland soils are often infertile.

Fig. 31 The influence of relief on soils

➤ Lowlands are warmer and usually flatter. This encourages the build-up of soil. Depending on the soil texture, they can be well drained. Biological activity is greater – earthworms and micro-organisms convert dead organic matter into humus. As a result, lowland soils are more fertile.

➤ Local variations in aspect and relief may cause some areas to be colder or wetter, creating zones of waterlogged and boggy lowland soils.

Factor 3: Parent material

Parent material affects soil characteristics.

➤ The type of rock that a soil develops from can influence its pH, colour, water content and texture of soils. The influences are summarised as follows:

(a) Igneous and metamorphic rocks tend to develop acidic soils. (pH)

(b) Sedimentary rocks can develop a variety of soils depending on rock type. For example, sandstone can produce acidic pale brown well-drained, sandy soils (pH, colour, water content, texture).

Fig. 32 Limestone and soil

➤ Limestone produces calcium rich dark-coloured soils, e.g. terra rossa soils (pH, colour, texture).

➤ Shale tends to produce dark grey, wet, clay soils (pH, colour, water content, texture).

➤ The parent material of a soil is not always rock. In Ireland the majority of Irish soils have developed on glacial deposits of boulder clay, sands and gravels. These soils tend to be deep, fertile and well drained.

Factor 4: Living things

Living things influence soil fertility.

➤ Living things within the soil can increase the fertility and **aeration** (the amount of oxygen) of a soil and can prevent soil erosion.

➤ Earthworms, beetles and insect larvae burrow through the soil and create air spaces for plant roots.

➤ Water can collect inside the burrows and keep the soil moist. When these creatures die, their bodies decompose and add nutrients to the soil.

➤ Micro-organisms such as fungi and bacteria add nutrients by decomposing dead material.

Fig. 33 The roots of even small seedlings can reduce soil erosion.

21

➤ Plant roots help to anchor the soil to the ground and prevent it from being blown away. Leaves and branches protect the soil from the impact of **rain-splash erosion** which in wet climates is very powerful and can remove tonnes of soil over a season.

Fig. 34 Burrowing earthworms are good for soil.

Factor 5: Time

The longer that the soil-forming processes listed above are in operation, the more developed the soil will become. Time allows soil to develop its characteristics fully in response to the processes that occur due to climate, relief, parent material and living things.

Factor: CLIMATE					
Temperature					Rainfall

Factor: TYPE OF WEATHERING					
Chemical					Mechanical

Factor: PARENT ROCK		
Metamorphic	Sedimentary	Igneous

Factor: PLANTS/ORGANISMS				
Increase humus content	Prevent soil erosion	Improve water holding capacity	Darken colour	Aerate the soil

PROCESSES AFFECTING SOIL						
Leaching	Humification	Podzolisation	Laterisation	Salinisation	Calcification	Gleying

SOIL CHARACTERISTICS						
Humus content	pH	Colour	Texture	Structure	Water content	Soil profile

Fig. 35 Summary table to show the relationship between factors affecting soil processes and soil characteristics.

questions

Chapter Revision Questions

1. List and describe the main constituents (ingredients) of soil.

2. Explain how soil forms. In your answer refer to:
    (a) Mechanical and chemical weathering
    (b) Plant growth
    (c) Micro-organisms

3. What is a soil profile? Draw a typical soil profile and label it.

4. Briefly describe the O, A, B and C horizons of a typical soil.

5. List the six characteristics found in all soils.

6. Make up a mnemonic to help you remember the six soil characteristics. (Note: A mnemonic is a memory tool. An example is the mnemonic for the colours of the rainbow; Richard Of York Gave Battle In Vain (Red, Orange, Yellow, Green, Blue, Indigo, Violet).

7. (a) Explain the term soil texture.
    (b) Name three soil textures.
    (c) Explain why loam soils are the optimum soil preferred by farmers.

8. Draw a table to summarise the characteristics of clay, silty and sandy soils.

9. (a) Explain the term soil structure.
    (b) Name three soil structures you have studied.
    (c) Draw a diagram to show each soil structure named in (b) above.
    (d) Describe each soil structure.

10. How does humus content affect soil? Refer to water content and fertility in your answer.

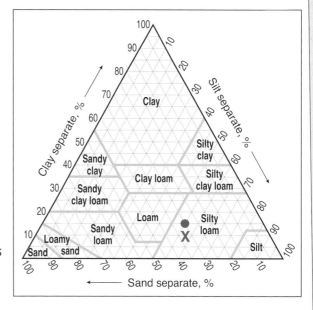

11. Using the chart above, classify soils with the following compositions:
    (a) 50% clay, 40% sand and 10% silt
    (b) 30% sand, 60% silt and 10% clay
    (c) 15% clay, 45% sand and 40% silt
    (d) Identify the composition of the silty loam soil at the point labelled X.

12. Name three nutrients important for plant growth and how they help the plant.

13. Why is the pH of a soil important for plants?

14. List three functions of water in soil.

15. Name and briefly explain the following soil-forming processes:
    (a) Humification
    (b) Leaching
    (c) Laterisation
    (d) Podzolisation
    (e) Calcification
    (f) Weathering
    (g) Salinisation
    (h) Gleying

16. Explain the impact of climate on soil formation.

17. Describe the impact of relief, parent material and time on soil formation.

Exam Questions

18. Examine the formation and texture of soils. [80 marks]

19. 'Soils can show a variety of texture and structure.'
Discuss this statement. [80 marks]

20. Examine the general composition and characteristics of any one soil type that you have studied.

[80 marks]

21. 'Soils have a variety of characteristics.'
Discuss this statement referring to four of the following:
(a) Colour
(b) Texture
(c) Structure
(d) Humus content
(e) Acidity/alkalinity
(f) Water content/retention

[80 marks]

22. Examine the factors that influence soil characteristics. [80 marks]
LC Exam Paper

23. Discuss the influence of parent material, climate and organic matter on soil formation. [80 marks]
LC Exam Paper

24. Examine two of the natural processes which influence soil formation.

[80 marks]
LC Exam Paper

Chapter 2
Soil Types

At the end of this chapter you should be able to:

- Describe in detail the brown earth soils of Ireland.
- Describe in detail either the latosols of Brazil or the aridisols of desert climates.

Contents

KEY THEME

Soils are affected by their immediate environment and by a combination of processes operating in that environment.

2.1 Irish brown earth soils

Soil type: Zonal

Ireland has a **cool temperate oceanic climate** and its natural vegetation is **mixed deciduous forest.** The zonal soil that develops in this climate is **brown earth soil.** Fig. 1 shows that brown earth soils dominate the soils of this country.

However, local conditions have modified the brown earth soil making **intra-zonal** soils that can be found in certain areas of Ireland. For example, waterlogging has created gley soils in County Monaghan and cool wet conditions after the last ice age prevented humification (rotting of plants into humus), thus allowing peat soils to build up in County Westmeath and County Offaly.

Mountain and hill blanket peat and podzolised soils
Mostly bare rock and rendzinas
Mainly blanket peat (low level and lithosols)
Basin peat
Mainly lowland gleys
Mainly acid brown earths and brown podzolics
Lowland gley brown podzolics and brown earths

Fig. 1 The variety of Irish soils

Fig. 2 Irish deciduous woodland

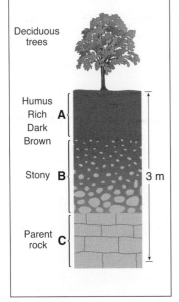

Fig. 3 Soil profile of Irish brown earth soils

Soil profile

This soil has no distinct horizons – it is uniformly brown in colour. This is due to the climate which encourages the presence and activity of living things such as worms and beetles within the soil. These mix the soil up and remove any horizons that may form due to leaching and humification.

Factors influencing brown earth soils in Ireland

1. Climate

The brown earth soil has developed in response to Ireland's cool maritime climate. This is a moderate climate. Temperatures range from 15°C in July to 6°C in January. Soil temperatures are rarely cold enough to stop biological activity completely. Rain falls throughout the year and amounts to an average of 1,500 mm per year. The climate encourages a long growing season and almost year-round bacteria, earthworm and fungi activity. Brown earth soils occur where the soil temperatures are above 0°C for 9 months of the year.

2. Relief

Relief influences the depth and drainage of this soil. Brown earth soils formed on slopes tend to be thinner and well drained. Mass movement creates deep soils at the base of slopes. Relief also affects temperatures. High ground is colder than lowlands because temperatures decrease by 1°C for every 100 m climb in altitude. In soils formed on colder higher ground there is less animal activity and less humus is formed than in soils formed on warmer lowlands. South-facing slopes have warmer soils than north-facing slopes so agriculture is often possible on soils found on slopes with a southerly aspect.

3. Living organisms/vegetation

The natural vegetation found over brown earth soils is temperate **deciduous forest**. These trees include oak, ash, chestnut and birch. They lose their leaves each winter adding valuable humus to the soil. Due to the mild climate micro-organisms such as fungi and bacteria are active for at least nine months of the year adding to the fertility of the brown earth soil. Animals such as badgers, rabbits and hedgehogs burrow into the soil churning it up, removing horizons and making the soil uniformly brown in colour.

4. Parent material

The parent material is varied. In many areas, its parent material is boulder clay deposited during the last ice age.

In Ireland, local changes to parent material have created three variations (intra-zonal) in brown earth soil:

(a) Acidic brown earths   **(b) Shallow brown earth (rendzina)**   **(c) Podzols**

(a) Acidic brown earth soils occur on land 500 m above sea level on crystalline rock such as granite, schist or sandstone, e.g. County Waterford.

(b) Shallow brown earth soils (also called rendzina soil) occur in limestone areas such as the Burren in County Clare and in County Sligo.

(c) Podzolised brown earth soils are slightly leached and occur on glacial drift of the Irish lowlands. This type of soil covers 22% of the country, e.g. County Dublin.

5. Time

These brown earth soils have developed since the last ice age over 10,000 years ago. They are mature well developed soils but have local variations depending on slope, aspect and drainage.

Characteristics of brown earth soil in Ireland

Colour

As its name suggests, brown earth soils are uniformly brown in colour. This is due to both the presence of humus, which makes it appear dark, and the action of leaching, which washes some nutrients out of the soil so that it is not too dark brown in colour.

pH

The pH of brown earth soil in Ireland varies from slightly alkaline to slightly acidic due to the temperate climate and variations in parent material (see page 27). Living things thrive in this kind of pH.

Bacteria, fungi, earthworms and spiders help to raise the fertility of the soil by drawing humus into the soil and decomposing it, releasing nutrients. The cool temperate climate is warm enough to allow biological activity to occur for more than nine months of the year.

Fig. 4 Autumn leaves add humus to brown earth soils.

Humus content

Brown earth soils are rich in humus because the natural vegetation that grows in the cool temperate climate is deciduous forest. These trees lose their leaves each autumn and the leaves add nutrients back into the soil as they are decomposed by fungi and bacteria.

Structure

The brown earth soil has a good crumb structure that provides pore spaces for air and water, encouraging plant growth. As a result of its crumb structure, Irish brown earth soils are highly productive and are used for tillage and pasture.

Texture

Brown earth soils generally have a loam texture due to the presence of a variety of parent materials such as sandstone, shale and alluvium from river flood plains (e.g. River Shannon).

Water content

This depends on local conditions of relief and drainage. Because of its generally loam texture and crumb structure, brown earth soils are not too wet or dry. They have a water content that encourages plant growth. The cool temperate oceanic climate provides 500 – 2,800 mm per year depending on relief.

Processes affecting formation of brown earth soil in Ireland

Humification

This soil is very fertile due to **humification**. The cool temperate oceanic climate encourages humification throughout the year. The rate of humification will decrease in winter and speed up in summer. The presence of large amounts of humus (autumn leaves and dead animals) adds to the soil's fertility.

Leaching

The year-round rainfall causes moderate amounts of leaching in brown earth soils. This adds to the fertility of the soil by gently washing nutrients down to the soil. Waterlogging can occur in poorly-drained areas causing brown earth soils to become gleys.

Fig. 5 Brown earth soil in an Irish strawberry field

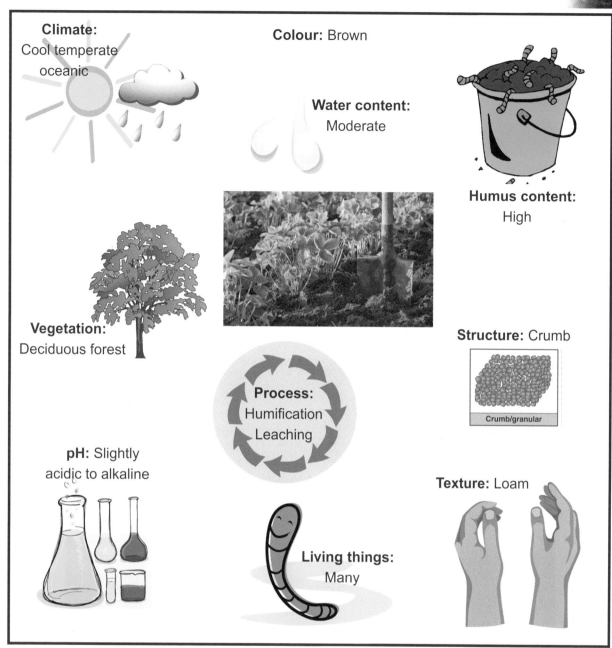

Climate: Cool temperate oceanic

Colour: Brown

Water content: Moderate

Humus content: High

Vegetation: Deciduous forest

Structure: Crumb

Crumb/granular

pH: Slightly acidic to alkaline

Process: Humification Leaching

Texture: Loam

Living things: Many

Fig. 6 Summary of brown earth soils

NOTE: You need to study either Section 2.2 or Section 2.3. If you intend to study the tropical rainforest biome in Chapter 4, you should study Section 2.2 (tropical latosols). If you intend to study the desert biome in Chapter 4, you should study Section 2.3 (aridisols).

2.2 Tropical latosols

Latosol – A tropical rainforest soil

Soil type: Zonal

Latosol soil is a zonal soil. It has developed in response to tropical and equatorial climates. These climates are hot (average 27°C), humid (88% humidity) and wet (up to 6,000 mm per annum) throughout the year.

Latosols are **red, heavily leached infertile zonal soils** that are found in the **tropical regions** of the world. They occupy 7.5% of the land area and cover large areas of South America, Africa and South East Asia. They are a major obstacle to the development of profitable agriculture in these regions. They are a fragile soil which can be easily damaged creating a useless laterite.

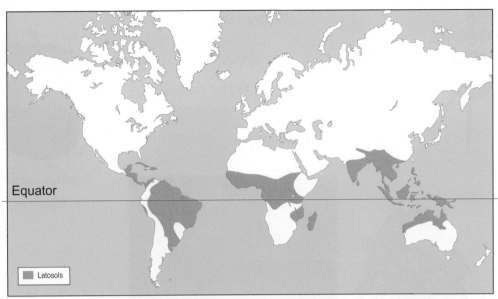

Fig. 7 Location of latosols in the world

Fig. 8 Forest clearance exposing latosols

Latosols support the richest vegetation on the planet – the **tropical rainforests**. Rainforests contain tall trees such as mahogany and teak. However, the latosol is not a fertile soil so how can such an infertile soil support such rich vegetation? The relationship between soil, climate and vegetation is possible due to the high rainfall and temperatures found in tropical regions. These conditions cause a short nutrient cycle. Plants grow rapidly, otherwise they will not get the nutrients before they are **leached** by the high rainfall.

If vegetation is removed, the soils quickly become infertile and vulnerable to erosion.

If the rainforest is cleared for agriculture, it will not make very good farmland as the soil will not be rich in nutrients and the soil becomes completely infertile within two or three years.

Soil profile

The latosol has a thin O horizon (humus layer) due to intense bacterial activity which rapidly decomposes dead organic matter.

The A Horizon contains aluminium and iron oxides. Sometimes iron and aluminium compounds build up in a hard layer lower down the profile.

The B horizon is very deep and uniform in texture due to intense leaching in high temperatures. Laterisation can reach many metres into the ground. These soils can be 40 m deep.

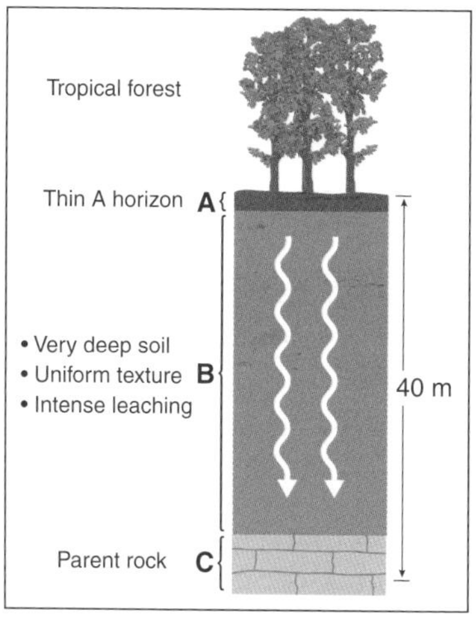

Fig. 9 Soil profile of a latosol

Factors affecting latosols

1. Climate

Because of their location in the tropics and equatorial regions of the earth, latosols form in very hot, wet conditions.

High rainfall, high humidity and high temperatures cause deep chemical weathering and rapid leaching of minerals down through this soil. Average rainfall is up to 3,000 mm (in some regions of Indonesia up to 6,000 mm of rain falls each year). Humidity is constantly high (88%) and the average temperature is 27°C. Because of the high temperatures and the permeability of the soil, heat and moisture reach great depths and rot the parent material into a deep soil. As a result latosol soils are very deep, e.g. 40 m in parts of Brazil.

2. Relief

These soils form under the rainforest on flat land and on slopes which allow tree growth. They are thicker on flat land and they are thinner and better drained where land is sloping.

3. Parent material

A variety of parent materials are found under latosols in Brazil. They range from metamorphic rocks to sedimentary limestone and river alluvium. These different parent materials cause the latosol to vary in colour from red to yellow and also influence its texture.

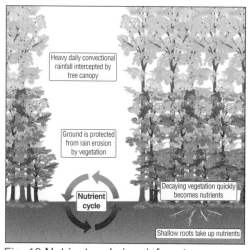

Fig. 10 Nutrient cycle in rainforest

4. Living organisms

The hot, damp conditions on the forest floor are perfect for fungi and bacteria to thrive and cause the rapid decomposition of dead plant material. This rapid humification provides plentiful nutrients that are easily absorbed by plant roots. However, as these nutrients are in high demand from the rainforest's many fast-growing plants, they do not remain in the soil for long and stay close to the surface of the soil. This cycling of nutrients is called the **nutrient cycle** and in latosols it is very short – a few days in some cases.

5. Time

Deep latosols result from the rapid weathering of parent material and the fast breakdown of organic material by fungi, bacteria and other living things which thrive in the hot, wet conditions of this region. Tropical regions were not affected by the last ice age and so have had many thousands of years to develop.

Characteristics of latosols

Colour

Latosols are red or yellow in colour. Leaching is so intense that only aluminium and iron compounds are left. These compounds give the soil its characteristic red or yellow colour.

Fig. 11 Laterite soil – note its hard surface.

pH

Due to the high rainfall the pH of latosols is moderately acidic. The rapid absorption of nutrients by vegetation growing in the soil helps prevent the latosol becoming more acidic. However once the forest is cleared, the latosol acidity rises.

Humus content

Latosols have a low humus content. This is due to the rapid breakdown of organic material by the many bacteria which thrive in the hot and wet conditions of this region and the equally rapid uptake of the humus by plants. Any humus formed is quickly absorbed by plants and does not make it below the O horizon of the soil.

Structure

Latosols lack a clearly defined structure. The structure of the latosol is often poorly developed due to the intense chemical weathering of mineral grains which prevents well shaped peds forming. Where the parent rock is granite, chemical weathering by hydrolysis causes clay minerals to form which give the latosols a platy structure.

Texture

Latosols may be any texture from loamy to clay to sandy. This is due to the variety of parent material and the fact that these soils lack silica. Latosols often show a combination of textures. Latosols formed on metamorphic or igneous rock tend to have a more sandy texture.

Water content

Latosols are wet due to high rainfall in the tropical region and are very permeable. However should the forest cover be removed this soil dries out rapidly and becomes impermeable to water and useless for farming.

Processes affecting latosol formation

Laterisation

Laterisation is the dominant process in forming latosols. Laterisation is a combination of deep leaching and chemical weathering by **carbonation, oxidation** and **hydrolysis**. Leaching and chemical weathering in the high temperatures of the tropics combine to dissolve all minerals except iron and aluminium oxides. These minerals give the soil its distinctive red/orange colour.

Due to the constant high temperatures, these soil-forming processes have reached deep into the ground and formed soils up to 40 m deep. Sometimes iron and aluminium compounds build up in a hard layer lower down the profile. If soil erosion removes the loose topsoil, the iron- and aluminium-rich lower layers are exposed. The high temperatures soon bake this soil into a hard bricklike surface which is impossible to cultivate even when wet. This type of soil is known as a **laterite**.

Humification

The hot, damp conditions allow for rapid humification which provides plentiful nutrients easily absorbed by plant roots. These nutrients stay close to the surface of the soil because they are quickly absorbed by the rainforest's many fast-growing plants.

Fig. 12 Nutrients stay close to the surface of the soil in tropical rainforests.

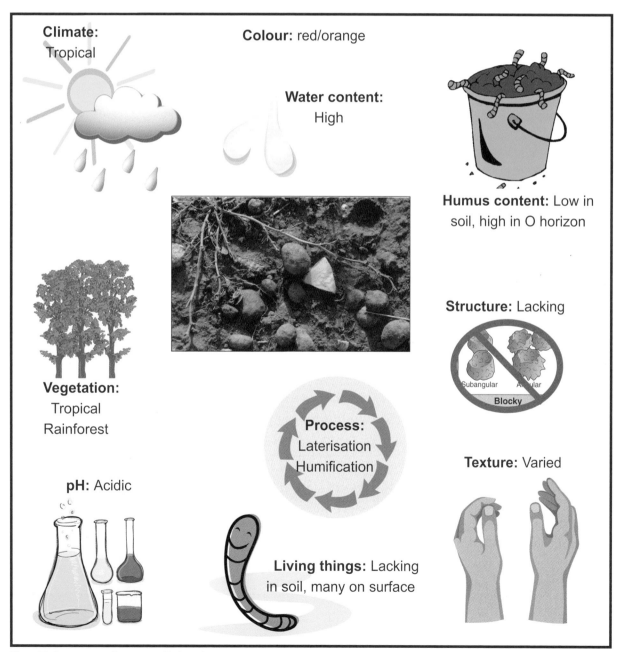

Climate: Tropical

Colour: red/orange

Water content: High

Humus content: Low in soil, high in O horizon

Structure: Lacking

Vegetation: Tropical Rainforest

Process: Laterisation Humification

Texture: Varied

pH: Acidic

Living things: Lacking in soil, many on surface

Fig. 13 Summary diagram of latosols

	Brown earth	Latosol
Zonality	Zonal soil, (cool temperate oceanic climate). Forms under deciduous woodland in temperate latitudes. Soil temperatures above 0°C for 9 months of year.	Zonal soil (tropical climate) rich in iron, alumina and silica forms in tropical woodlands in a very hot, humid climate. If deforested turns into hard laterite.
Main process	Humification	Laterisation
Humus content/ fertility	High: micro-organism activity high due to temperate climate	Low: lacks humus. Leaching is so intense that plants absorb any nutrients rapidly so they do not get carried into the soil. Nutrients provided by rapid decomposition of organic matter in hot climate.
Colour	Brown	Orange/yellow/red
Horizons	No distinct horizons due to mixing of soil by living things such as worms	Thin A horizon, deep B Horizon (40 m); Hard pan sometimes present
Texture	Loam	Varies depending on local conditions. Often loamy sand texture.
Structure	Crumb	Varies according to main soil constituent – can be blocky or platy.
pH	Slightly acidic to slightly alkaline depending on parent rock.	Acidic

Fig. 14 Table to compare/contrast Irish brown earth soils and tropical latosol soils.

NOTE: You need to study either Section 2.2 or Section 2.3. If you intend to study the tropical rainforest biome in Chapter 4, you should study Section 2.2 (tropical latosols). If you intend to study the desert biome in Chapter 4, you should study Section 2.3 (aridisols).

2.3 Aridisols – A hot desert soil

Soil type: Zonal

Aridisols have developed in response to the desert climate. This is a dry, (less than 250 mm of rain per year) hot climate. Hot deserts usually have a large **diurnal** temperature range, with high daytime temperatures (45 °C) and low night-time temperatures (0°C). Humidity is low.

Hot deserts occur between 15° and 40° north and south of the equator at coasts and interiors of continents. There is a huge variety of desert soils. In this section we are going to focus on one type of desert soil – the **aridisol**. These soils occur in hot desert areas of the world. See Fig. 16 in Chapter 4, page 62. Hot deserts are found in North Africa, California, Australia and South America and in the Middle East.

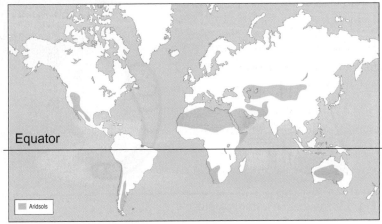

Fig. 15 Location of aridisols in the world

Aridisols are soils rich in calcium carbonate. Because of the dry climate in which they are found, they are not used for agricultural production unless irrigation water is available. Aridisols occupy 12% of the earth's land area.

Soil Profile

Aridisols show some horizon development. They may develop surface pebble layers called **desert pavement**.

Fig. 16 Aridisols occur in the desert biome.

They contain horizons in which clays, calcium carbonate, silica, salts and/or gypsum have accumulated. The A horizon is light in colour as there is little vegetation to add organic matter to the soil profile.

Aridisols may contain whitish layers called **calcic horizons**. These are accumulations of calcium carbonate, the same material found in chalk, concrete and agricultural lime. They form due to the process of calcification. Calcic horizons may vary from 15 cm to 1 m in thickness and form an impermeable, cement-like layer or **hard pan** in the soil known as **caliche**.

Factors affecting aridisols

1. Climate

Aridisols form in arid and semi-arid regions in the world. These areas have little or no rainfall. Annual rainfall is less than 250 mm in arid places and up to 250-500 mm in more semi-arid regions. Generally desert precipitation occurs in short violent showers of rain and is totally unpredictable.

The sun is high overhead and skies are cloudless producing temperatures that range from between 20°C and 45°C down to below freezing at night. The bare rock and sand absorbs this intense heat. At night, the heat built up over the day is quickly lost into the atmosphere due to the absence of clouds. Temperatures drop very quickly.

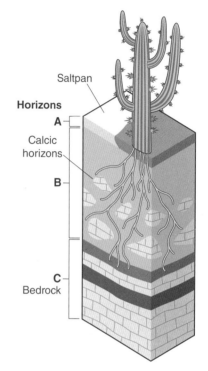

Fig. 17 Aridisol soil profile

This climate causes intense mechanical weathering especially **exfoliation** creating angular scree particles for soil formation. The lack of rainfall prevents chemical weathering from occurring. Strong winds and sand storm can often remove very fine sand particles leaving coarser and heavier soil particles behind.

Fig. 18 The desert climate is the most important factor affecting aridisol formation.

2. Relief

Relief has a major influence on aridisols. Valleys provide pathways for flash floods (the valleys are known as **waddis** in Arabia and Africa) which remove soils in the valley floors. Water flowing off mountainsides deposits mud, sand and gravel at the base of the slopes in huge fan-shaped deposits called **alluvial fans**. These alluvial fan sediments are an important parent material for aridisol soil and influence the texture and mineral content in soils nearby by providing sand, silt and clay particles.

Fig. 19 Relief influences the depth and texture of desert soils.

3. Living things/vegetation

Vegetation is scarce or almost completely absent, unless it has specifically adapted to this harsh environment. The plants that do thrive are mainly ground-hugging shrubs and short woody trees such as Yucca, Agaves, Cactus and Mesquite shrubs which have adapted to the dry conditions by storing water.

There is rapid growth in vegetation after the unpredictable torrential downpours of rain. Plants and animals are closely linked with many animals and insects using the plants as shelter and food sources. But this scarce vegetation cover is very limited and restricts the soil-building properties of micro-organisms that could convert the organic matter into humus. Consequently aridisols are mineral rich but lack humus.

4. Parent material

In desert soils parent material is quite varied. In some areas of the south-west USA, parent material is gravelly alluvium derived from old granite rocks. This parent material has influenced the colour of the soil here where it is dark red with white caliche deposits.

5. Time

Desert soils that have developed on older parent material are redder in colour than soils developed on younger materials which are often pale grey.

Characteristics of aridisols

Colour

Some aridisols have the same pale, brownish colour from top to bottom, but others may be layered with browns, reds, pinks, and whites. The variation in colour is due to the action of living things, salinisation, weathering and parent material.

pH

Aridisols have high calcium carbonate and sodium concentrations making them alkaline.

Humus content

Aridisols contain little organic matter. This is caused by the low plant productivity, which in turn restricts the soil-building properties of micro-organisms that convert organic matter into humus.

Structure

Aridisols have a blocky structure and may also have a platy structure where the clay content of the soil is higher.

Texture

Aridisols have a coarse sandy or gravelly texture because there is less chemical weathering. The finer dust and sand particles are blown elsewhere, leaving heavier pieces behind. Coarse textured soils are found on lower mountain slopes and are fairly well drained. In lower-lying basin areas finer particles have been blown and accumulated creating a deep well-drained soil cover.

Water content

Aridisols are characterised by being dry most of the year and with limited leaching. The low water content is also related to the low humus content because soils with a low organic matter content have a low water-holding capacity – they cannot retain all the water that falls onto them.

Processes affecting aridisols

Calcification

Calcification is responsible for the formation of the chalk-rich hard pan or caliche within aridisol soils. Water is drawn up through the soil pores by capillary action driven by evaporation of water from the surface. Calcium carbonate is deposited in layers in the soil or near the surface. This hard pan makes the soil hard and difficult for plant roots to break through.

Salinisation

The intense evaporation of water from desert soils tends to bring dissolved salts to the surface. The high surface content of sodium and calcium ions can lead to extensive hard surface crusts of salt (**saltpans/salinas**) where little or nothing can grow because the salt is toxic to plants. Farmers need to break up this hard pan and dilute the salt with irrigation water to get the soil into production. In some countries the salt pans are put into commercial production for table salt.

Fig. 20 Salinised soil prevents vegetation growth in desert regions.

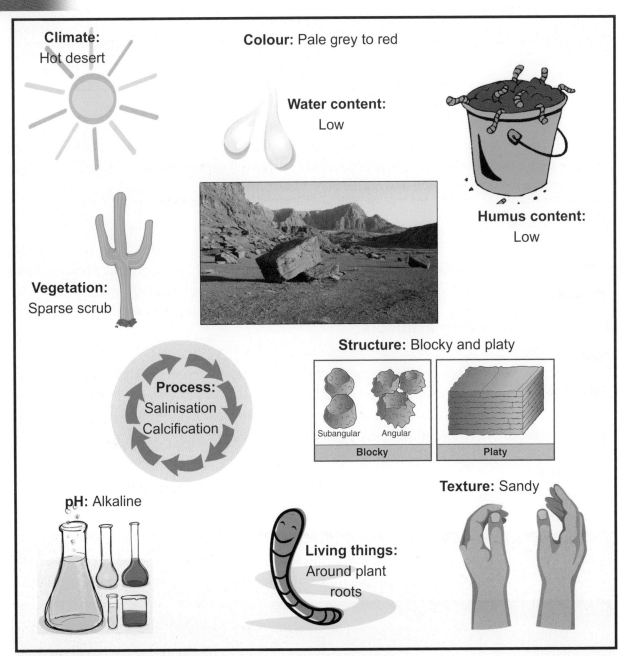

Climate: Hot desert

Colour: Pale grey to red

Water content: Low

Humus content: Low

Vegetation: Sparse scrub

Process: Salinisation Calcification

Structure: Blocky and platy

Subangular   Angular
Blocky   **Platy**

pH: Alkaline

Living things: Around plant roots

Texture: Sandy

Fig. 21 Summary diagram of aridisols

Fig. 22 Hot desert landscape in the south-west USA

	Brown earth	Aridisol
Zonality	Zonal soil, (cool temperate oceanic climate). Forms under deciduous woodland In temperate latitudes. Winter temperatures above 0°C for 9 months of year.	Zonal soil (desert climate). Rich in calcium carbonate and sodium carbonate.
Main process	Humification	Salinisation and calcification
Humus content/ fertility	High: micro-organism activity high due to temperate climate.	Low: lacks humus due to absence of vegetation and micro-organisms caused by dry conditions.
Colour	Brown	Pale brown, red, pink or white.
Horizons	No distinct horizons due to mixing of soil by living things such as worms	Some horizons but not always well developed. May contain caliche/hard pan horizon.
Texture	Loam	Coarse, sandy, gravelly.
Structure	Crumb	Can vary – may be blocky and/or platy.
pH	Slightly acidic to slightly alkaline depending on parent rock.	Alkaline

Fig. 23 Table to compare/contrast Irish brown earth soils and hot desert aridisol soils

Fig. 24 Hot desert landscape in north Africa

questions

Chapter Revision Questions

1. (a) What are zonal soils? Give an example.
    (b) What is an azonal soil? Give an example.
    (c) What is an intra-zonal soil?

2. Describe Irish brown earth soils. What processes have led to variations in this soil type?

3. Draw a labelled soil profile of a brown earth soil.

4. Describe the characteristics of latosols **or** aridisols.

5. Draw a labelled soil profile of a latosol **or** an aridisol.

6. Draw a summary table to show the similarities and differences between brown earth soils and **either** latosols **or** aridisols. Use the headings:

    (a) Colour
    (b) Depth
    (c) Soil processes
    (d) Climate/location
    (e) Fertility

Exam Questions

7. Compare and contrast the characteristics of any two soil types which you have studied.
    [80 marks]

8. Describe and explain the characteristics of any one soil type studied by you.
    [80 marks]
    LC Exam Paper

9. With reference to one soil type you have studied, examine how parent material, climate and organic matter influence the soil.
    [80 marks]
    LC Exam Paper

10. Examine the general composition and characteristics of any one soil type that you have studied.
    [80 marks]
    LC Exam Paper

Chapter 3
Soil Erosion and Conservation

At the end of this chapter you should be able to:

- Name and explain the causes of soil erosion.
- Describe in detail how human activities can cause soil erosion.
- Name and explain the primary methods of soil conservation.

Contents

KEY THEME

Soil erosion is a challenge facing many countries. Human activities can cause soil erosion but several methods can be used to prevent it.

3.1 Soil erosion

Soil is a fragile resource. Once it is eroded, it is not renewed. Conservation of soil fertility and the prevention of soil erosion are challenges that face millions of people if their future food supplies are to remain secure.

Throughout the world, soil erosion is a serious problem. Most soil erosion is caused by natural processes such as water flowing downhill and by the wind. It can happen on slopes with as little as a 10 cm drop in a 20 m length. Human activities such as overcropping and overgrazing land and deforestation also cause soil erosion.

Each year the US loses about two billion tonnes of topsoil. In China, the loss of soil is a serious threat to that country's future food supply. The loss of valuable topsoil due to wind and water erosion in the tropical lands of Africa is one of the greatest problems this continent faces.

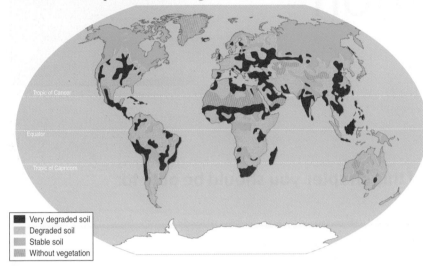

Very degraded soil
Degraded soil
Stable soil
Without vegetation

Fig. 1 Degraded soil areas of the world

Natural causes of soil erosion

Soil erosion by rain and wind

Raindrops on average fall at a speed of 32.19 km/h. The force of the impact of raindrops breaks apart the soil grains. The larger the raindrop, the greater the energy released at impact and thus the more destruction of the soil occurs. During heavy rain so much rain falls, water can no longer seep into (infiltrate) the soil. Therefore it begins to flow over the surface. This is called **runoff**. The water

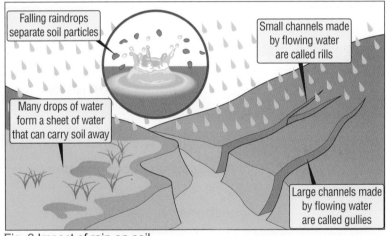

Falling raindrops separate soil particles

Small channels made by flowing water are called rills

Many drops of water form a sheet of water that can carry soil away

Large channels made by flowing water are called gullies

Fig. 2 Impact of rain on soil

then makes channels called rills and gullies in the soil. Millions of tonnes of soil are removed from farmland by rainwater in this way.

Wind is very effective at blowing dry exposed soil away. Wind removes soil by:

(a) Saltation - fine and medium sand-sized particles are lifted a short distance into the air, dislodging more soil as they fall back to the ground.

(b) Suspension - very fine soil particles are lifted from the surface by the impact of saltation and carried high into the air, remaining suspended in air for long distances.

(c) Surface creep - the movement of large soil particles along the surface of the soil after being loosened by the impact of saltating particles.

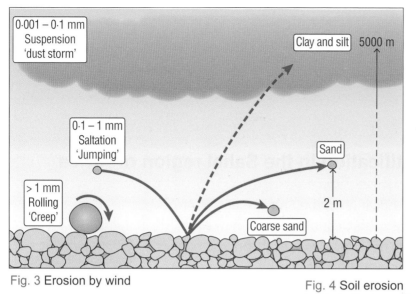

Fig. 3 Erosion by wind

Fig. 4 Soil erosion leads to the loss of productive farmland.

The amount of soil erosion by wind and rain that occurs depends on:

1. The **quantity of water** moving downhill, e.g. more water = more erosion
2. The **speed of the water**, e.g. faster flow = more erosion
3. The **strength** of the wind
4. The **steepness** of slope
5. The **condition of the soil surface** and the type of soil, e.g. few plants, dry, compacted soil leads to more erosion.

Human causes of soil erosion

Humans have an important impact on soils. Human influence can trigger soil erosion due to poor farming methods and deforestation. Both farming and deforestation change soil characteristics and can damage the soil structure. In many regions of the world, human activities such as overgrazing, overcropping and deforestation have led to desertification, soil erosion and famine.

Tourism in mountainous areas can also lead to the loss of soil as it is carried away on the boots of thousands of hillwalkers, e.g. in the Alps and Himalayas. Other outdoor activities, e.g. scrambling and quad biking, also damage the fragile soil structure and are banned in many mountainous areas of the world.

The amount of soil erosion caused by human activities depends on:

1. The **type of cultivation** – may leave soil exposed to wind
2. The **amount of vegetation cover removed** – deforestation can lead to landslides
3. The **intensity of land use** – heavily used soils are more easily eroded
4. The **length of time land left fallow (rested)** – overused soils are often dry.

Problems caused by soil erosion

1. Loss of valuable topsoil. When topsoil is removed from a field it includes the soil particles, soil nutrients, water and water-holding capacity.
2. Poor soil washed downhill can bury valuable fertile soil on the lowland below.
3. Damage to fields because gully erosion reduces the field size and takes land out of production.

4. Erosion causes a steady but slow plant productivity decline. For example, if 10 cm of soil is removed from a field, it would have a 5-15% decline in productivity.

5. Desertification.

Soil erosion and desertification in the Sahel region of Africa

Soil erosion is leading to desertification in the Sahel region of Africa. Desertification is the spread of desert conditions into new areas. It occurs in areas close to existing deserts. However, it can also happen in well-watered areas if the climate changes and becomes drier and human activities create conditions leading to soil erosion.

Soil erosion and its resulting desertification have two main causes:

1. **Human activities** such as overgrazing, overcropping and deforestation, generally triggered by population growth.

2. **Climate change** – global warming is increasing drought conditions in certain areas of the world.

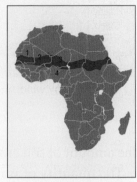

Fig. 5 The Sahel region of Africa. Name the countries 1-6.

Fig. 6 An overgrazed landscape

Fig. 7 This soil is too dry and compacted for food production to occur.

1. Human activities

In the Sahel region, soil erosion is occurring largely as a result of the human activities of **overgrazing, overcropping** and **deforestation**. These activities lead to **soil degradation** and desertification.

(a) **Overgrazing** occurs when farmers allow too many animals to graze an area of land. This damages soil structure and removes plant cover, allowing the soil to blow away.

The population of the Sahel region has grown, including the numbers of farmers. As a result, the number of cattle and goats on the land has increased. Overgrazing by cattle has become a major cause of soil erosion in the Sahel. Large herds graze the land and their hooves compact the soil destroying its structure. With more animals grazing the land the soil structure gets damaged and young trees and shrubs are destroyed by the grazing animals. This reduces soil humus and removes the roots necessary to anchor the soil to the ground. Continued grazing also removes the protective cover of grasses increasing the risk of erosion.

As nomadic farming in the Sahel continues to be replaced with more settled farming, farmers have constructed enclosures for cattle and goats so the land becomes intensively grazed.

Fig. 8 Watering livestock borehole in southern Ethiopia

Fig. 9 Goats are good climbers and can forage in trees leading to deforestation.

(b) **Overcropping** occurs when land is continuously farmed. This drains nutrients from the soil and destroys the soil structure making it less fertile. The soil becomes dry, dusty and is easily removed by wind erosion and rain.

Overcropping is also caused by population growth. The growing population needs more food from the already weakened soil. Despite improvements in farming methods, in some areas of the Sahel the land is being overcropped, i.e.

Fig. 10 Large herds of goats contribute to overgrazing

the land is not left to rest between crops and/or is not fertilised properly.

Another reason why overcropping occurs in the Sahel region is the poor economic situation in many Sahelian countries. Many Sahelian nations availed of cheap loans from developed nations during the 1960s, but are now having trouble repaying these loans. They become **Highly Indebted Poor Countries** (HIPCs). To qualify for debt relief, governments in the Sahel have to increase the amount of land under cash crops such as cashew nuts and cotton. These are grown on huge plantations and sold on the international market to pay off national debts. The plantation land is intensively cultivated as a **monoculture**. The same crop is grown each year depriving the soils of particular nutrients which in most cases are not replaced. The land can become sterile and useless.

The plantation workers live on and use land on the edges of the plantations to grow their own food crops leading to overcropping and overgrazing in these areas.

Fig. 11 Cotton cash crop plantation in Africa

case study

The land around the edges of crop plantations is continuously in use. It cannot be left fallow to regain its nutrients as people would go hungry. The soil becomes overcropped, dry and dusty and is blown or washed away. Therefore, growing cash crops allows desertification to encroach onto the plantations themselves.

(c) **Deforestation** occurs when large areas of forest are cut down, leaving a bare landscape. Forests provide natural protection for soil from rain and wind preventing mass movement.

Tree and plant roots anchor the soil, preventing soil erosion. When the trees and shrubs are removed the soil (formerly protected and sheltered by the trees) dries out due to constant exposure to the sun and is easily blown away or washed away in flash floods and landslides.

As the population rises, more trees are felled for building materials and for firewood because the people cannot afford any other fuel. They may not have the money to replant more trees.

Once the trees have been cleared, cattle dung, which was once left on the land to fertilise it, is now used as a fuel for cooking. This removes a source of valuable fertiliser increasing the risk of soil erosion.

The combination of overgrazing, overcropping and deforestation means that the lack of nutrients and destruction of soil structure renders the soil useless for future farming. Land is abandoned and over time the desert spreads onto these once productive farmlands.

The soil is also becoming drier due to the increasing demand for water for human and animal consumption and for irrigation. More wells are sunk and this, along with climatic changes, is causing the water table to drop.

Due to the destruction of the soil, the region is now classed as **overpopulated** as it cannot feed its population.

Fig. 12 Wood cut for fuel contributes to deforestation.

2. Climate change

Global warming has changed the pattern of rainfall in the Sahel. It is causing a rise in the temperature of the atmosphere. As a result the air can hold more water vapour and condensation/precipitation is less likely to occur.

The seasonal rains are becoming less reliable. Rainfall levels have decreased by as much as 30% over the last 20 years in the region. In parts of Sudan the amount of rain decreased from 720 mm per year (similar to the east of Ireland) to 440 mm per year. Droughts are therefore becoming more frequent and lasting longer. As a result, the soil is drying out and becoming exposed to erosion. Desertification is continuing.

1.	In the Sahel region, population growth has led to an increase in cattle numbers on the land. This has reduced plant cover and compacted the soil. (Overgrazing)
2.	Wells have been dug to provide water for cattle. Around the bore holes, so many cattle gather that the land is ruined over many hectares.
3.	Plantation owners put huge areas of land under cash crops. This forces people to cultivate the land more often. Fields are not left to rest between crops. The soil loses nutrients and becomes useless. (Overcropping).
4.	Rising populations create a demand for fuel wood. This further deprives the soil of important humus and increases soil erosion.
5.	Drier climate due to climate change.

Fig. 13 The above factors combine to cause soil erosion which leads to desertification in the Sahel.

3.2 Methods of soil conservation

Soil conservation involves the protection and maintenance of soil to avoid soil erosion. Soil conservation aims to continue the productive life of soil indefinitely. Proper management of this vital natural resource is necessary if soil is to remain a sustainable resource.

Soil conservation methods include:
1. Windbreaks/shelter belts
2. Contour/strip ploughing
3. Stubble planting
4. Terraces
5. Stone walls or bunds
6 Reduce ploughing in dry/windy weather

1. Windbreaks

One important form of soil conservation is the use of windbreaks. Windbreaks are barriers formed by trees and other plants with many leaves, e.g. switchgrass. They are planted around the edges of fields on areas of land that are exposed to wind. Windbreaks stop the wind from blowing soil away. They also prevent the wind from destroying or damaging crops. They are very important for growing grains, such as wheat. Windbreaks can protect areas up to ten times the height of the tallest tree in the windbreak.

Fig. 14 Windbreaks prevent soil erosion in large fields.

In parts of West Africa, studies have shown that grain harvests can be 20% higher on fields protected by windbreaks compared to those without such protection.

Windbreaks seem to work best when they allow a little wind to pass through. If the wall of trees and plants stops wind completely, then violent gusts occur close to the ground. These gusts lift the soil into the air where it will be blown away. To avoid this, there should be at least two lines of plants in each windbreak. One line should be large trees. The second line can be shorter trees and other plants.

Windbreaks not only protect land and crops from the wind, they can also provide wood products. These include wood for fuel and fences. Locally grown trees and plants are best for windbreaks as they are adapted to local conditions.

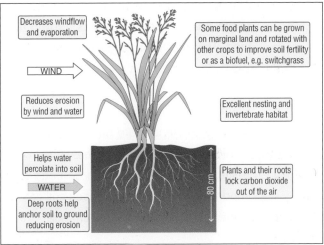

Fig. 15 Switchgrass plants work very well as windbreaks.

2. Contour ploughing/strip ploughing

With contour ploughing, the tractor operator follows the contours of a hillside, i.e. they go around the sides of the hills following the contours of the hillsides. This technique is more troublesome and potentially dangerous than the old method of going straight up and down the hillsides.

However, in terms of preventing soil erosion, the benefits of this technique are enormous. The furrows thrown up by the plough will now act as 'mini terraces', slowing or stopping the flow of rainwater and encouraging it to percolate into the soil.

By ploughing straight up and down the hillsides, the furrows act as ditches, enabling the water to flow down them picking up speed and soil. This fast-flowing mixture of water and soil increases the size of the furrow, deepening it until it reaches the harder subsoil below. Meanwhile, many tonnes of life-sustaining topsoil are carried away to the sea.

Contour ploughing is widely used in Europe and North America.

Fig. 16 A contour ploughed field

Fig. 17 The crop stubble is left in place when new crop is planted.

3. Stubble planting

For centuries, the old stubble of crops harvested in a year was ploughed back into the soil.

Using the stubble planting method, the old stubble of harvested crops is not ploughed back into the soil. Instead the stubble is left in place. This is suited to many of the grain and cereal crops planted in Ireland.

Any fertilisers and new seed planted afterwards are inserted into the soil through small slits cut into the soil by a razor-type device attached to the tractor. In other words the soil is left virtually undisturbed. The stubble will reduce wind and water erosion while the new crop is growing. It also gives cover and habitat to small birds.

The stubble left on the soil will rot into the soil eventually, increasing the humus content as it would have when ploughed in. Stubble planting is used in the prairie lands of America and Canada. It is also used in Europe.

4. Terraces

Terraces are large steps cut into a hillside to make flat land for agriculture. Terraces work by reducing slope length and steepness to limit the energy of running water and its ability to carry soil away. Stopping or slowing the downhill flow of water allows the sediment to drop out of the water onto the terrace adding soil to the terrace. This prevents gully erosion.

Terracing is used in Asia.

Fig. 18 Terracing on a hillside in Thailand.

5. Stone walls or bunds

These low walls are placed along the contour of a hill and capture water, allowing it to filter into the soil rather than running off downhill. These walls are about one metre high and are a very simple way of preventing soil erosion on a slope. Stone walls are used in India.

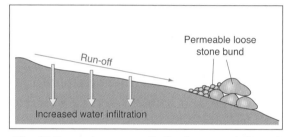

Fig. 19 Bund slows run-off allowing percolation of water into soil

6. Reduce ploughing in dry/windy weather

Not ploughing when the soil is dry and dusty reduces the risk of wind erosion. This is very important, because soil is lost during the ploughing process (see Fig. 20) and it is also lost if the following days are windy with no rain to dampen and settle the fine soil particles. This is used in North America.

Fig. 20 Ploughing in windy weather increases soil erosion.

Chapter Revision Questions

1. How do wind and rain cause soil erosion?

2. List three human activities that can lead to soil erosion.

3. Describe how the following factors influence the occurrence and speed of soil erosion:
   (a) Water
   (b) Soil type

4. Explain the terms:
   (a) Desertification
   (b) Overgrazing
   (c) Overcropping
   (d) Deforestation

5. Describe how human activities have led to soil erosion in the Sahel region of Africa.

6. How has climate change affected rainfall levels and patterns in the Sahel region of Africa?

7. Explain the terms contour ploughing and stubble planting.

8. Name and describe three methods used to prevent soil erosion. Draw labelled diagrams to illustrate your answer.

Exam Questions

9. Discuss how human activities can accelerate soil erosion.
   [80 marks]
   LC Exam Paper

10. Examine the causes of soil erosion and outline methods used to prevent it.
    [80 marks]

11. Examine how overcropping/overgrazing and desertification can affect soils.
    [80 marks]
    LC Exam Paper

12. Examine two ways in which human activities have impacted on soils.
    [80 marks]
    LC Exam Paper

Chapter 4
Biomes

At the end of this chapter you should be able to:

- Explain the term biome.
- Describe in detail one major biome in terms of its climate, soil, plants and animals.
- Explain how animals and plants adapt to their biome.

Contents

NOTE: You are required to study **ONE** biome.
You may choose either 4.2 The tropical rainforest biome **OR** 4.3 The hot desert biome.

KEY THEME

The pattern of world climates has given rise to distinctive biomes. These biomes are world regions characterised by groups of plants and animals which have adapted to specific conditions of climate, soils and biotic interrelationships.

4.1 Biomes

Biomes are unique natural world regions which are controlled by climate. Examples of biomes include the tropical rainforest biome, the deciduous forest biome, the desert biome and the tundra biome.

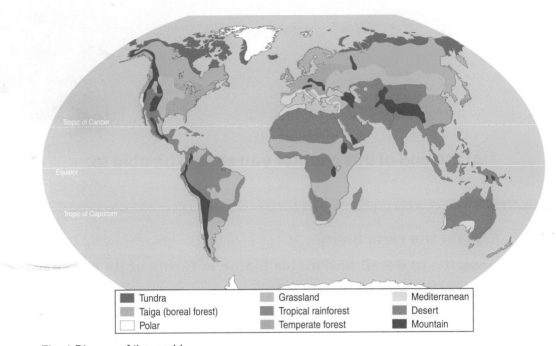

■ Tundra	■ Grassland	■ Mediterranean
■ Taiga (boreal forest)	■ Tropical rainforest	■ Desert
□ Polar	■ Temperate forest	■ Mountain

Fig. 1 Biomes of the world

There are four parts in any biome: **climate**, **soil**, **plants** and **animals**. These parts are interdependent.

Climate is the most important factor affecting a biome.

Climate determines what type of soil is formed there, what plants grow there and which animals inhabit it.

The soil develops in response to the climate, then plants evolve and grow in response to the climate. The humus provided by the plants affects the development of the soil. Animals evolve to cope with the conditions provided by the climate, soil and plants. Plants and animals develop inter-relationships with each other in order to survive the climatic and soil conditions in the biome.

Animals and plants have evolved body parts and ways of living to enable them to survive in their biome. This is called **adaptation**.

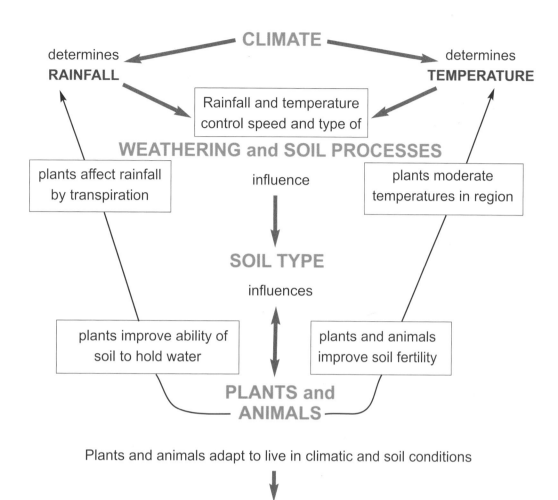

Fig. 2 The relationship between **climate**, **soil**, **plants** and **animals** in any biome

4.2 The tropical rainforest biome

The tropical rainforest is a forest of tall trees found in the hot, wet, tropical zone around the earth. It is also known as the jungle.

The tropical rainforest biome is home to the greatest variety of living things (**biodiversity**) on the planet. This biodiversity is due to its tropical climate which is warm, sunny and humid all year, providing perfect conditions for the growth of plants and animals. The tropical rainforest biome is an important part of the global climate system. It produces water vapour and absorbs carbon dioxide from the atmosphere. Tropical rainforests also produce about 30% of the world's fresh water through transpiration.

Fig. 3 The tropical rainforest is a forest of tall trees.

Covering less than 2% of the earth's surface, rainforests are home to about half of all living things on the planet.

> It is estimated that a typical patch of rainforest measuring just 6 km² contains as many as 1,500 species of flowering plants, 750 species of tree, 400 species of bird, 150 species of butterfly, 100 species of reptile and 60 species of amphibian.

Rainforests provide many useful **foods and materials**, e.g. bananas, citrus, peppers, cashews, peanuts, coffee, tea, cocoa, vanilla, sugar and spices.

Fibres from tropical forests are used in rugs, ropes, string and fabrics. Tropical forest oils, gums and resins are found in insecticides, fuel, paint, varnish, cosmetics, shampoos, perfumes and disinfectants.

Life-saving medicines such as quinine (malaria), aspirin (pain relief) and two-thirds of all medicines found to have cancer-fighting properties come from rainforest plants.

Location of the rainforest biome

The tropical rainforest biome is found in the tropical zone between 23.5° north and 23.5° south of the equator.

The main areas are:

1. Central America and the Amazon Basin.
2. The Africa-Congo basin, with a small area in West Africa and in eastern Madagascar.
3. Indo-Malaysia – off the west coast of India, Southeast Asia, New Guinea and Queensland, Australia.

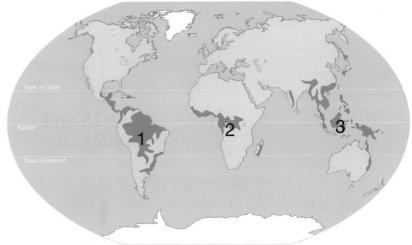

Fig. 4 The rainforest biome

Key characteristics of the rainforest biome: Climate

- The climate in this region is tropical, which means it is hot, wet and humid all year.
  This is because in the tropics, sunlight strikes the earth at roughly a 90° angle and the region receives almost 12 hours of sunlight every day. This results in intense heating. The average temperature is about 27°C. There is a small temperature range. Day length hardly changes between summer and winter. The sunlight is converted to energy by plants. Since there is a lot of sunlight, there is a lot of energy locked up in the rainforest. This energy is stored in plants that are eaten by animals.
- Due to the intense heating large amounts of moisture evaporates from the ground and vegetation. Water vapour rises, cools and condenses to form heavy **convectional rainfall** each day. An average of 1,250 mm to 6,600 mm of rain falls in a rainforest each year. This leads to high humidity levels with average humidity between 77% and 88%.
- Rainforest climates are very different from other environments. In other climates, the water vapour blows away and later falls as rain in far off areas. But in rainforests half the precipitation comes from the forests' own evaporation. This is because each tree might release over 755 litres of water every year by **transpiration** and this falls back to the land as rain.
- The tropical climate is responsible for the great variety of living things in the rainforests.
- Plants grow very well and there is plenty of food for animals.

Soils

- The **latosol** is the zonal soil associated with the tropical rainforest biome. (See Chapter 2, pages 29-34.) Rapid, deep chemical weathering and leaching play an important role in its formation. The latosol is very poor in nutrients. Thousands of years of heavy rains have washed the nutrients away by the process of leaching. If nutrients are not in the soil where are they?

  Nutrients are found mainly in living plants and in the layer of decomposing plant material on the ground surface (the O Horizon). A study in the Amazon rainforest found that 99% of nutrients are held in the root mats of the forest floor.

- Various species of **decomposers** such as insects, bacteria and fungi make quick work of converting dead plant and animal matter into humus (humification).

  So there are few nutrients deeper in the soil because plants intercept and take up nutrients from the O horizon the moment they are released by humification. If they did not do this, the nutrients would be quickly leached from the soil by the heavy rain.

  Therefore, rainforests have a very short **nutrient cycle**. It takes a few days for dead organic matter to be converted into humus and absorbed by plant roots. All life in the rainforest is based on decay.

- When a rainforest is burned or cut down, the source of the nutrients is removed from the biome. The soil in the destroyed rainforest can only be used for a very short time before it becomes completely depleted of all its nutrients.

  Poor soil management such as deforestation, intense heat and heavy rainfall can lead to **laterite** soils developing. Laterite is a hard brick-like soil impossible to cultivate, even when wet. It is caused by the high temperatures that bake the exposed soil into a hard impermeable material which is often used for building blocks.

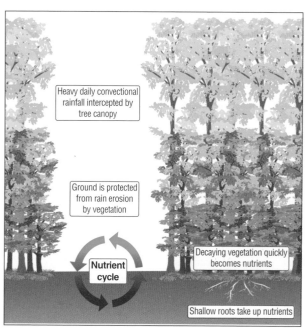

Fig. 5 Rainforests have a very short nutrient cycle

Vegetation

- There is a great variety of vegetation in the rainforest. Each of the three largest rainforests (the South American, the African and the Asian) has a different plant group and animal species. However, their plant species look very similar and in many cases the trees can only be identified by their flowers. Typical rainforest trees include teak, mahogany, palm oil and brazil nut trees. It can take 60 years for a tree to grow large enough to cut.

- As you have read, the tropical region receives 12 hours sunlight per day and conditions are hot and humid. This is perfect for plant growth.

- To avoid **competition** with each other for light and moisture, the plants have evolved a unique four-layered structure consisting of the **emergent layer**, the **canopy layer**, the **understorey layer** and the **forest floor layer**. This four-layered structured is due to the climate. Each plant is adapted to survive in a particular layer. This allows thousands of plants to live together and use the sunlight available in each layer. See Fig. 6.

1. Emergent layer

The emergent layer consists of the tops of the tallest trees, which range in height from 40 m to 80 m. It contains birds like the scarlet macaw, insects and many other creatures. In the emergent layer trees are spaced far apart with umbrella-shaped outlines that grow above the forest. Because emergent trees are exposed to drying winds, they tend to have small, pointed leaves. These giant trees have straight, smooth trunks with few branches. Their root system is very shallow, and to support their size they grow buttresses that can spread out to a distance of more than nine metres.

2. Canopy

The canopy is the name given to the upper parts of the trees which grow below the emergent layer. The canopy is found 20-40 m above the ground. This leafy environment is full of life: insects, spiders, many birds like the toucan and the hornbill. There are mammals such as the orang-utan and the howler monkey (the second-loudest animal in the world after the blue whale).

The canopy is home to snakes, lizards and frogs. Plants in the canopy include thick, snake-like vines and **epiphytes** (air plants) like mosses, lichens and orchids which grow on trees.

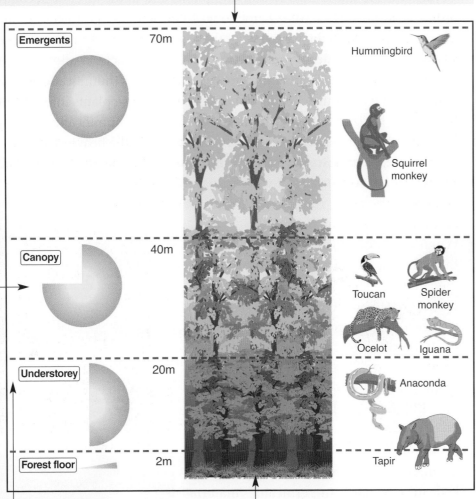

3. Understorey

The understorey is a dark environment that is under the canopy. Most of the understorey of a rainforest has so little light that plant growth is limited. There are short, leafy, mostly non-flowering shrubs, small trees, ferns and vines (lianas) that have adapted to filtered light and poor soil. Animals in the understorey include insects (like beetles and bees), spiders, snakes, lizards, and small mammals that live on and in tree bark. Some birds live and nest within tree hollows. Some larger animals, like jaguars, spend a lot of time on branches in the understorey, looking for prey.

4. Forest floor

The floor of the forest is teeming with animal life, especially insects and spiders like tarantulas. The largest animals in the rainforest generally live here, including gorillas, anteaters, wild boars, tapirs and jaguars. Indigenous people also live in the forest, e.g. the Yanomami of Brazil. Less than 3% of the light that strikes the top of the forest penetrates to the forest floor so the forest floor is often completely shaded, except where a tree has fallen and created an opening. The forest floor receives so little light that few plants can grow there. As a result, a person can easily walk through most parts of a tropical rainforest. The top soil is very thin and of poor quality. A lot of leaf litter falls to the ground where it is quickly broken down by termites, earthworms and fungi. The heat and humidity further help to break down the litter. This organic matter is then quickly absorbed by the trees' shallow roots.

Fig. 6 Layers of trees in a tropical rainforest showing amount of sunlight received and common animals

Animals

- A tropical rainforest contains more than 100 different species of animal in each hectare. The South American rainforest, particularly around the Amazon Basin, contains a wider variety of plant and animal life than any other biome in the world. There are nearly 30 million different species of insects, 1,600 species of bird, more than 2,500 species of fish and 2,500 different species of tree in the Amazon.

- Different rainforests may have different species, e.g. gorillas are found only in African rainforests, orang-utans only in Indonesian rainforests and jaguars only in South American rainforests.

- Insects make up the largest single group of animals that live in tropical rainforests. They include brightly coloured butterflies, camouflaged stick insects and thousands of species of ants and beetles.

- Each species of animal has evolved to live in a particular rainforest layer.
  Most rainforest animals live in the canopy layer. Few move between layers and many never touch the ground at all e.g. the flying squirrel and tree frog.
  Because of their tree-living (**arboreal**) lifestyle, most animals are small.

Fig. 7 Hummingbirds, proboscis monkeys and jaguars are rainforest animals.

Plant and animal adaptations to the rainforest biome

As so many plants and animals live in the rainforest, there is great competition for soil nutrients, food and sunlight amid the wet humid conditions. Plants and animals have therefore developed special features in order to survive in this environment. This is called **adaptation**.

Plant adaptations to climate and soil

In order to survive in the hot, wet and sunny tropical climate and the infertile latosol soils, rainforest plants have made many adaptations to their environment. The adaptations can be grouped under three headings:

      1. Leaves   **2. Roots and trunks**   **3. Parasitic plants**

1. Leaves

- The climate is wet, warm (27°C) and humid (88% humidity). Plants must cope with large amounts of water falling onto their leaves each day (30 mm of rain per day) and with fungal attack in the warm humid conditions.

- Plants have made adaptations that help them shed water off their leaves quickly so the branches don't get weighed down and break. Many plants have flexible leaves that bend easily.

- Others have holes and drip tips. Many have grooved leaves to channel water to their roots. Some leaves have oily coatings to repel water and resist fungal attack.
- As less than 3% of the sunlight reaches the forest floor, leaves are very large to absorb as much light as possible. In the canopy where there is more wind, leaves are smaller, narrower and pointed to reduce drying. Plants have adapted to the lack of sunlight by growing large leaves when just a sapling on the forest floor and then growing smaller leaves as they mature and reach the canopy.

Fig. 8 This tropical plant leaf has holes to help it shed water and a waxy surface to repel it.

2. Roots and trunks

- Trees have straight trunks that do not branch until a height of 30 m or more. This is because there is no need to grow branches below the canopy where there is little light.
- The high level of sunlight in the tropical climate encourages plant growth. Emergent layer trees such as mahogany have evolved to grow extremely tall to win the competition for light.
- However, they must also cope with an infertile latosol soil which has all its nutrients close to the soil surface. So they have **shallow root systems**.
- In order to support the tall tree and to gather nutrients the roots fan out over the surface and form **buttress roots**. Other trees grow their roots down from branches to the ground to support themselves. These roots are called **Stilt roots**. (See Fig. 9.)

Fig. 9 Stilt roots on a rainforest tree

- The majority of the trees have smooth, thin bark because there is no need to protect them from water loss and freezing temperatures. It also makes it difficult for plant parasites to get a hold on the trunks.
- Many plants in the upper regions of the rainforest have aerial (air) roots. They are called **epiphytes**. The roots use the moisture in the air. Their sponge-like roots gather water and soak it up for later use. Plants like orchids, bromeliads and ferns have this type of root system. They grow high in the canopy and the roots never reach the ground. Many fleshy fruits are produced. These large fleshy fruits attract birds insects and animals to help disperse their seeds.

3. Parasitic plants

- Parasitic plants live off the nutrients supplied by their host plant or they use them for support. **Vines** or **lianas** are a good example. Over 2,500 species of vines or lianas grow in the rainforest.
- Lianas have adapted to the dark conditions on the forest floor by 'catching' a tree and using it for support, taking a lift to the light. Lianas start off as small shrubs that grow on the forest floor. They send out tiny shoots or tendrils to grab sapling trees and grow with them to reach the sunlight of the upper canopy. The liana and the young tree grow towards the canopy together. Lianas turn into strong woody vines which can grow from one tree to another and may make up 40% of the canopy leaves.

- **Strangler figs** use a different technique. They start as epiphytes growing on a canopy tree and send their roots down to the forest floor. Their seed is dropped in a nook at the top of a tree and starts to grow, using the debris collected there as nourishment. Gradually the fig sends aerial roots down the trunk of the host, until they reach the ground and take root. As it matures, the fig will gradually surround the host, criss-cross its roots around the trunk and start to strangle it. The fig's branches will grow taller to catch the sunlight and its roots rob the host of nutrients. Eventually the host will die and decompose leaving the hollow trunk of the strangler fig.

Fig. 10 A strangler fig has killed its host tree.

Animal adaptations to the climate and soil

- Tropical rainforests are almost perfect for animal survival. It is always warm and there are no seasons of food scarcity. There is shade from the heat and shelter from the rain. There is no shortage of water.
- However, because there are so many creatures living in the rainforest, there is a great deal of competition for food and space. To avoid overcrowding while feeding, creatures have adapted by foraging for food by night (nocturnal) or only during the day.
- Animals have adapted indirectly to the climate and soil by becoming experts at living in tall forests which grow in response to the climate and soil in tropical regions. Each animal has adapted to living in a particular forest layer.

The adaptations can be grouped under the headings:

    1. Camouflage/colour   **2. Body structure**   **3. Animal-plant relationships**

1. Camouflage/colour

- Camouflage is one of the most effective adaptations used by a wide variety of animals. One of the most common and effective types of camouflage is looking like a leaf or twig. The rainforest floor is scattered with dead leaves so animals and insects often use camouflage to look like dead or living leaves and are very hard to see from above. Moths, **stick insects**, chameleons and tree frogs use this method.
- Other animals such as the **jaguar** have spotted coats to blend into the shaded forest. Animals also use colour to warn predators that they are poisonous. Some of the brightly-coloured animals are just bluffing. However, the **poison arrow frog** is most definitely not bluffing. This frog comes in many different colours – from sky blue to black and green. Poison arrow frogs get their name from rainforest tribes who use the secretions from their skin to poison the tips of their blow-gun darts.
- **Sloths** are covered with a greenish layer of algae which camouflages their fur in their tree-living (arboreal) environment. Sloths also move very slowly, making them even harder to spot. They may spend the whole of their life on one tree.

Fig. 11 A poison arrow frog

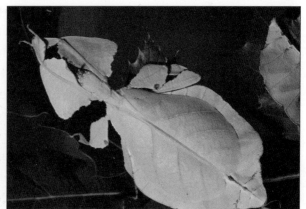

Fig. 12 An insect camouflaged as a leaf

2. Body structure

- Because the tropical climate and latosol soil has produced a layered forest of tall trees, many animals must adapt to living in trees. They travel between trees and must be good climbers or fliers.
- **Flying squirrels** have evolved flaps of skin between their front and back legs. This allows them to jump between the trees and glide for longer distances than they would normally be able to leap.
- Having a tail that can wrap around a tree branch (a **prehensile tail**) is another useful adaptation seen in animals such as **lemurs** and **spider monkeys**. The proboscis monkey has a large nose, allowing its warning calls to be louder than other monkeys.
- Some animals can flatten their bodies onto a tree bark for protection against predators, e.g. **gecko lizard**.
- The hooked beaks of macaws and other parrots allow them to easily open nuts. They also use their beaks as an extra foot when climbing.
- Some animals like the sloth have hooked claws to help grip the branches they hang from. They have large eyes in order to see in the shady environment. Their fur grows down from their body unlike other animals so that it can shed water as they hang upside-down from tree branches.

Fig. 13 Black spider monkey with prehensile tail

Fig. 14 Young sloth: Note fur on legs, hooked claws and large eyes.

3. Animal–plant relationships

- To avoid competition for food in the tropical climate some animals have became very **specialised**. This means that they adapted to eating a specific plant or animal that few others eat. There is a close relationship between plants and animals in the forest. Animals depend on plants for a home and food. In turn, plants depend on animals to fertilise and disperse their seeds.

- The **Ceiba tree** is covered in vivid red flowers that attract many insects and hummingbirds, who drink the nectar, collect pollen and fertilise the tree. Some species of frog live on only one species of tree. The humidity levels enable them to live away from ponds and rivers and to lay eggs in trees.
- **Parrots** and **toucans** eat nuts and have developed big strong beaks to crack open the tough shells of Brazil nuts. **Leafcutter ants** climb tall trees and cut small pieces of leaves which they carry back to their nest. The leaf pieces they carry are about 50 times their weight. The ants bury the leaf pieces, and the combination of the leaves and the ants' saliva encourages the growth of a fungus, which is the only food these ants eat.

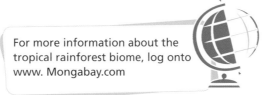

For more information about the tropical rainforest biome, log onto www. Mongabay.com

4.3 The hot desert biome

Deserts cover about one fifth of the Earth's surface and occur where rainfall is less than 500 mm per year.

There are four types of desert:

(a) hot and dry

(b) cold and dry

(c) semi-arid

(d) coastal

In this section we will focus on the **hot desert biome**.

Most hot deserts have a considerable amount of specialised vegetation, as well as specialised animals and insects. The soils are often rich in mineral nutrients. They just need water to become very productive but they have little or no organic matter. Sudden infrequent but intense rains may cause flash flooding.

There are relatively few large mammals in deserts because most are not capable of storing sufficient water and coping with the heat. Deserts often provide little shelter from the sun for large animals. Mammals are usually small, like the kangaroo mice of North American deserts.

Fig. 15 Large ears help the jackrabbit to cool down. Its pale brown fur help to camouflage it from predators such as coyotes.

Location of the hot desert biome

Hot deserts are found between 15°–30°north and south of the equator.

Hot deserts can be found in the following regions:

1. The Sahara Desert in Africa
2. The Californian Desert in the south-west USA
3. The Thar Desert in north-west India and Pakistan
4. The Australian desert
5. The Atacama Desert in Chile, South America
6. The Namib and Kalahari Deserts in Africa

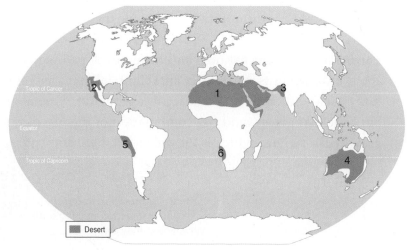

Fig. 16 Location of hot desert biomes

Key characteristics of the desert biome: Climate

Hot deserts have low rainfall, i.e. less than 250 mm per year. They have a very high rate of evaporation (seven to fifty times as much as precipitation), and a wide daily (**diurnal**) range in temperature. Hot desert temperatures range from 0°C at night to 45°C during the day.

The dramatic temperature changes are the result of the low **humidity**. The lack of moisture prevents clouds forming. This allows up to 90% of solar radiation to travel through the atmosphere and heat the ground during the day. At night the heat is released back into the atmosphere because there are no clouds to trap it.

A combination of the following factors leads to the dry desert climate.

Factors causing desert climate

1. **Latitude:** Desert regions are found at the tropics (15° – 30° north/south of the equator). This area is under the influence of a global high pressure belt. The year-round high pressure means air sinks to the ground and warms up all the time. Due to the heat there are very low levels of moisture in the atmosphere, making it very dry. See Fig. 19 on page 63.

2. **Dry prevailing winds:** Hot deserts lie in the path of dry trade winds. These winds warm up as they blow towards the equator from the sub-tropical high pressure belts. They absorb moisture rather than form rain clouds so the air is clear and dry.

3. **Cold Ocean Currents**: Some deserts on the western edges of continents (Atacama in Chile, Great Victoria in Australia, Kalahari and Sahara in Africa) are located beside cold ocean currents, e.g. the Canaries Current. These currents cool the prevailing winds that travel across the oceans triggering rainfall over the sea. By the time the winds reach the land they are dry.

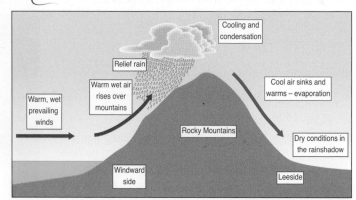

Fig. 17 Some hot deserts lie in the rainshadow of high mountains.

4. **High mountain ranges:** Some deserts are dry because of the **rainshadow** effect of high mountain ranges such as the Rocky Mountains of America. Prevailing winds rise over the mountains triggering relief rain on high ground. The land in the sheltered lee of the mountains receives very little rain as the air descends, e.g. the south-west USA deserts.

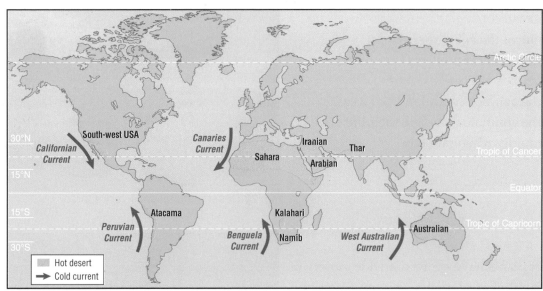

Fig. 18 Ocean currents lead to desert conditions.

Due to the combination of factors above, hot deserts usually have very small amounts of highly irregular rainfall. The average rainfall is 150 mm a year. Rain usually comes in short violent storms three to fifteen times a year. On average, only one to six of these rainfalls are large enough to stimulate plant growth.

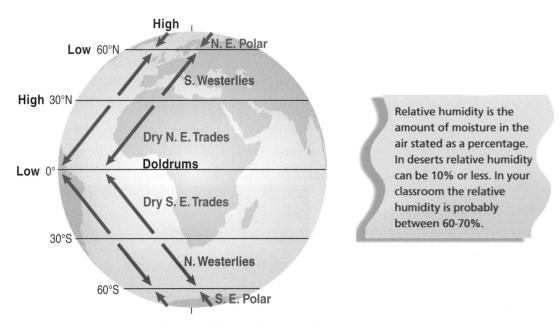

Relative humidity is the amount of moisture in the air stated as a percentage. In deserts relative humidity can be 10% or less. In your classroom the relative humidity is probably between 60-70%.

Fig. 19 Deserts lie in the path of dry NE and SE Trade Winds.

Vegetation

- Desert vegetation is very **sparse**. Plants are almost all ground-hugging shrubs and short woody trees. Some examples of these kinds of plant are Turpentine Bush, Prickly Pears and Brittle Bush. For all of these plants to survive they have to **adapt** to the climate and soil.
- Some of the adaptations are:
  - the ability to store water for long periods of time
  - the ability to withstand hot weather
  - the ability to complete their life cycle rapidly when rain falls

Fig. 20 Desert vegetation is very sparse.

Desert plants have evolved a wide variety of structural characteristics to store water and limit the amount of water they lose – from dense spines on some cacti that create shade for the plant underneath to a waxy coating on the surfaces of leaves.

Fig. 21 Desert plants such as cactus plants can store water and limit the amount of water they lose.

Soils

- The zonal soil of the hot desert is the **aridisol** (see Chapter 2, page 34-39).
- Desert soils tend to be poorly developed with a high content of mineral particles from the stony parent material but little organic matter. This is caused by the low plant productivity, which restricts the soil-building properties of micro-organisms that convert organic matter into the humus components of soils.
- The soil directly beneath the plants that do grow is enriched with organic matter and nutrients, compared to bare areas between plants.
- The main process affecting this soil is **salinisation**. Desert soils tend to have extensive areas of **salt pans**.
- Some desert soils allow deep soakage of water; others have an impermeable hard pan or caliche layer that prevents the soil holding much water at depth.

Fig. 22 Desert soils are often stony and lack humus.

Animals

- Most desert animals are **generalists** and **opportunists**, animals that eat whatever they find, whenever they can find it. Small animals are more common in desert regions, e.g. coyote, jackrabbit, desert toad and kangaroo rats.
- Very few large mammals live in deserts. They cannot cope with the heat and lack of water. Many animals are nocturnal to avoid the extreme daytime heat. They live in burrows during the day and come out at night to feed when it is cooler.
- Beneath plants, organic materials are buried by the burrowing activities of mammals. Dead plant roots provide abundant organic matter on which many small animals feed. Each plant is a 'fertile island' and fosters higher densities of small animals living on and in the soil.
- Very small spiders and microscopic worms live in the soil close to plant roots. Animals range in size from microscopic mites and worms to snakes, badgers and coyotes.

Plant and animal adaptations to desert biome

Because of the extremely hot and dry climate in this biome, plants and animals have developed special features in order to survive in this environment. This is called **adaptation**.

Plant adaptations to climate and soil

The availability of water is the single greatest limitation to plant life in deserts. The amount of moisture that is available for plants to use is dependent on the soil. Some soils have horizons that allow deep infiltration of water; others allow water to seep only a few millimetres into the soil. Various **perennial** (plants that live for several years) plant species respond differently to these contrasting soil moisture conditions, e.g. the mesquito bush. Some species are better suited to soils that foster deep infiltration of moisture; others have ways to cope with the extreme seasonal fluctuations of shallow soil moisture.

In order to survive in the desert climate and soil, plants have adapted in four ways:

1. Store water	**3. Fast life cycles**
2. Tap root and shallow root systems	**4. Bloom at night**

1. Storing water

Desert plants have developed ways of storing water in their leaves, stems and roots to survive the dry conditions. These plants are called **succulents**, e.g. **cactus** plants.

In order to store water for months on end, succulent plants have developed several ways to reduce the amount of water they lose through evaporation through their skin.

These are:

- Thick waxy leaves and dense hairs that prevent moisture loss.
- Sharp, thorny leaves that prevent birds, insects and animals from biting into the plant to get at their water.
- A dense coating of hairs (**trichomes**) slows air moving over the surface of the plant. Since air in the desert is very dry, any air movement tends to increase evaporation. The trichomes create a layer of humid air around the plant reducing water loss.
- The ability to expand when water is available. The plants have thick grooves which direct water to the roots and enable the plant to fill up during rainfall, e.g. the barrel cactus.

Fig. 23 The thorns on cactus plants prevent animals from eating them.

Fig. 24 A barrel cactus has spines and grooved, waxy skin to conserve water. It also has shallow roots.

Fig. 25 Saguaro cactus has shallow roots and a spongy interior for storing water.

2. Tap roots and shallow root systems

Some desert plants such as cacti have relatively **shallow fibrous root systems** which spread out over large areas to capture as much water as possible when it rains. They are capable of quickly using shallow soil water when it is briefly available and then surviving lengthy periods when it is not.

Other plants have long **tap roots** that reach deep into the soil in order to reach the permanent **water table**. The location of these plants depends on the soil. Not all desert soils allow water to seep deep underground. For example, the location of the **creosote bush** in deserts is closely related to the soil moisture. The creosote bush is found in desert soils that allow deep infiltration of water. It has adapted by evolving a deep root system that enables it to extract water from deep underground. Although the creosote bush also contains abundant shallow roots, the availability of the more constant deeper supplies of water allows this evergreen shrub to remain active throughout the entire year, even during extended rainless periods when shallow soil moisture has largely disappeared.

Fig. 26 Creosote bush has tap and shallow roots to maximise moisture.

Shallow roots capture soil moisture near the surface

Tap roots capture deep soil moisture

Fig. 27 The creosote bush is well adapted to desert soils.

3. Fast life cycles

Many desert plants have evolved to cope with the dry climate by completing their life cycle in just a few weeks after rain has fallen. These plants are called **ephemerals**.

These plants produce seeds that can survive in a **dormant** state for many years while they wait for rain to fall and trigger germination into a new plant. When rain falls, the seeds quickly grow into new plants, flower and produce new seeds and then die in the space of three or four weeks, e.g. the desert poppy and Cereus plant (desert Dandelion).

4. Bloom at night

In order to avoid the drying heat of the daytime, some plants such as the Cereus plant open their flowers at night. This reduces water loss and also increases their chances of pollination as many insects and small mammals are nocturnal too.

Animal adaptations to climate and soil

Animal adaptations to the hot desert climate can be grouped into four categories:

1. Adaptations to avoid daytime heat.
2. Adaptations to cool their bodies down in the hot climate.
3. Adaptations to absorb water.
4. Adaptations to conserve water.

1. Avoiding daytime heat

In order to survive in the hot desert climate many desert animals are **nocturnal**, e.g. the **kangaroo rat**. They hide in burrows or under rocks during the day and are most active searching for food and water at dawn and dusk. This lifestyle avoids the sun at its full daytime strength. Insects and small mammals move around plants to stay in the shade.

Other animals **hibernate** underground for long periods and emerge to the surface only when there is rain. The amazing desert **spadefoot toad** can spend several years in a dormant state buried in muddy holes underground. They lie underground waiting for the vibrations of rain hitting the surface.

Fig. 28 The spadefoot toad can hibernate for years waiting for rain to complete its life cycle.

When they sense rain, they go the surface, mate and lay eggs which quickly develop into tadpoles and then toads. This happens in as little as 14 days. Once the ground dries out, they dig a hole and hibernate in a water-filled cocoon until the next rain falls.

2. Adaptations to cool their bodies down in the hot climate

Keeping cool in the hot desert climate is very important for desert animals. The **camel** keeps its fat reserves in a hump on its back so that it can keep cool more easily (unlike whales and dolphins who have a thick layer of fat all over their bodies in order to keep warm in the cold sea).

The camel is an unusual desert animal because it is large. Most desert animals are small and their bodies lose heat more rapidly. Some of them have developed long body parts that provide greater body surface to dissipate heat. For example, **jackrabbits** have large upright ears that are supplied with a large number of blood vessels from which excess heat can be easily lost.

Light colours are better reflectors of heat than dark colours and most desert animals are pale in colour. This prevents their bodies from absorbing more heat from the sun and is also a camouflage against predators.

In the Australian desert, **kangaroos** lick their forearms to make them wet. As the saliva evaporates it cools the blood close to the skin surface and enables the kangaroo to survive the hot temperatures.

Fig. 29 Kangaroo rats can manufacture water from the digestion of dry seeds.

Fig. 30 Camels are able to drink 100 litres of water at a time. Camels also have long eye lashes and extra eyelids to protect them from desert dust storms and can close their nostrils independently to protect their lungs from dust. They have large pads on their feet to stop them sinking in the sand.

3. Adaptations to absorb water

Desert animals are experts at getting as much water from their environment as possible. Kangaroo rats are known to be able to manufacture water from the digestion of dry seeds. Many desert rodents have extra blood filter tubes in their kidneys that help them to extract most of the water from their urine and return it to the bloodstream. They also filter the moisture out of their exhaled breath through specialised organs in their nostrils.

Camels are able to drink over 100 litres of water at a time and they do not sweat. This means that they can last two months without water.

4. Adaptions to conserve water

Many desert animals conserve water by not passing urine out of their bodies, e.g. snakes. They get all the water they need from insects and plants. They excrete dry pellets, e.g. kangaroo rats. Others store water in fatty tissue in their bodies, e.g. the **Gila Monster**, a type of poisonous lizard who can store water in the fatty tissues in its tail. The fat in the camel's hump will produce water and energy when it is used by the camel when food is scarce.

Fig. 31 A Gila Monster and a cactus: both animal and plant are able to store water.

Impact of soil on desert animals

Soil conditions directly affect where many kinds of desert animals live. For burrowing animals, the choice of a place to excavate a living shelter may depend on soil texture. For example, in the Mojave Desert in the USA, desert tortoises require soils that are loose enough to be excavated, but firm enough so that the burrows will not collapse. Consequently, in areas containing both extremely sandy soils and loamy soils with higher clay content, tortoises prefer to construct their burrows in the loamy soils.

Different kinds of soil horizons may prevent the burrowing activities of some animals. For example, the mound-like burrows of the kangaroo rat frequently are found beneath the canopy of a large creosote bush in sandy to loamy soils that lack substantial development of calcic horizons. However, on soils with extremely shallow, strongly cemented calcic horizons, this species of kangaroo rat is usually absent or rare, probably because of the difficulty of excavating burrows in these soils.

Fig. 32 Tortoises usually build their burrows in loamy soils.

Impact of animals on desert soils

Animals in turn have an effect on desert soils. The animals that dig, wriggle, tunnel and burrow through desert soils range in size from microscopic mites to jackrabbits, snakes and coyotes. Their activities move soil around and cycle nutrients between soil and plants.

The soil directly beneath perennial plant canopies is enriched with organic matter and nutrients, compared to bare areas between plants. Beneath plant canopies, organic materials are buried by the burrowing activities of mammals, and dead plant roots provide abundant organic matter on which many small animals feed. Plants are therefore 'fertile islands' which encourage higher densities and increased activity of small animals living on and in the soil.

Chapter Revision Questions

1. Explain the term biome. Name two biomes.

2. Draw an outline map of the world. Show the equator and the locations of the tropical rainforest biome.

3. Describe the climate of the tropical rainforest biome.

4. Name and describe the soil of the tropical rainforest biome.

5. Name the four layers of vegetation in the tropical rainforest biome.

6. Briefly describe the plants and animals found in each layer.

7. Describe how plants and animals have adapted to live in the tropical rainforest biome.

8. Describe the tropical rainforest biome under the headings:
   (a) Location
   (b) Climate
   (c) Vegetation
   (d) Adaptations of plants and animals to the climate and soil.

9. Draw an outline map of the world. Show the equator and the locations of the hot desert biome.

10. Describe the climate of the hot desert biome.

11. Name and describe the soil of the hot desert biome

12. Describe how plants and animals have adapted to live in the hot desert biome.

13. Describe the hot desert biome under the headings:
    (a) Location
    (b) Climate
    (c) Vegetation
    (d) Adaptations of plants and animals to the climate and soil.

Exam Questions

14. Describe and explain the main characteristics of a biome that you have studied.

    [80 marks]
    LC Exam Paper

15. Illustrate the development of biomes, with reference to a specific example.

    [80 marks]
    LC Sample Paper

16. Discuss the interaction between climate, vegetation and soil in a biome that you have studied.

    [80 marks]

17. Examine the adaptations of plants and animals to conditions in a biome that you have studied.

    [80 marks]

18. Describe how plant and animal life adapt to soil and climatic conditions in a biome which you have studied.

    [80 marks]
    LC Exam Paper

19. Examine the influence of climate on the characteristics of one biome that you have studied.

    [80 marks]
    LC Exam Paper

Chapter 5

The Impact of Human Activities on Biomes

At the end of this chapter you should be able to:

- **Provide detailed examples of how people have changed biomes through their settlement, agricultural and industrial activities.**

Contents

KEY THEME

Biomes have been changed by human activities.

A variety of human activities have changed biomes across the world. These activities include:

1. Settlement
2. Deforestation
3. Intensive agriculture
4. Industrial activity

5.1 The impact of early settlement and the clearing of the deciduous forest biome in Ireland

Clearance of native Irish deciduous forest

Since the last ice age ended the natural vegetation of Ireland has been deciduous forest. This forest grew in response to the cool temperate climate that developed since that ice age.

Trees such as oak, ash, birch and elm once covered over 70% of Ireland. Animals such as the wolf and red squirrel were common throughout the country.

Continual settlement from prehistoric times to the mid-twentieth century reduced this woodland cover dramatically and caused a decline in native animal and plant species. Overall the impact of settlement has been to clear the native deciduous forest biome and affect two of its iconic animals – the wolf and red squirrel. Over centuries it has been replaced with a landscape of managed agricultural grass and croplands. Non-native coniferous tree plantations have been established for commercial use.

- **Prehistoric times (5,000 – 6,000 years ago)**: A deciduous mixed woodland biome covered much of the landscape of Ireland. The most common trees were oak, elm, ash, Scots pine and alder.

  Between 5,000 and 6,000 years ago, the first farmers began to clear woodlands to create farm land. Prior to this, there was only a small population of New Stone Age farmers and their **stone tools** took time to make and were not very strong. As a result, forest clearance was confined to small areas.

- **Iron Age (600 BC – AD 500)**: With the development of bronze and iron, forest clearance increased. Iron Age people had sharp and strong **metal axes** which increased both the area of land that could be cleared for settlement and farming and the speed at which this clearance took place. From roughly 600 BC to 500 AD, the amount of woodland in Ireland began to decrease. Some trees and woodland plants were protected by the **Brehon law**. The most important trees in Irish forests were the so-called **nobles of the wood** oak, hazel, holly, yew, ash, Scots pine and crab-apple. Under Brehon Law, any person who damaged one of these trees had to pay a fine of two milk cows and one three-year-old heifer.

Fig. 1 The invention of bronze and iron axe heads increased deforestation in Ireland.

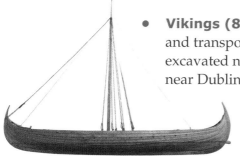

- **Vikings (800 – 1000):** The Vikings used wood to build settlements and transport (e.g. longboats) in Ireland. One Viking longboat excavated near Copenhagen was built in about 1060 from Irish oak cut near Dublin.

Fig. 2 Wood from Irish trees was used to build many Viking longboats.

- **Normans (1100 – 1400):** The Norman settlement increased the amount of forest cleared. Timber was required by the Normans to construct bridges and defensive settlements.

   In addition, English planters began to arrive in Ireland from the 1500s onwards, which furtheraccelerated tree clearances due to the need for timber for building and industry. Planters also exported timber to supply the demand for wood in England.

   The population of Ireland was twice what it is today, so there was also a greater amount of timber used for fuel. Most of the remaining Irish oak forests were cleared at this time.

- **Plantations (1500 – 1700):** The native animal and plant species of the deciduous forest biome were affected by forest clearance, hunting and the introduction of new species during Plantation times. The introduction of new species of plants in the eighteenth century affected some native Irish plant species. Decorative Rhododendron plants were brought from Asia and Spain and spread into native forests in Cork and Kerry. It is a highly invasive shrub damaging the growth of natural woodland.

   Throughout most of the first half of the seventeenth century, Ireland had a substantial **wolf** population, possibly as high as 1,000 wolves. Wolves had been in Ireland throughout the last glaciations and are an important part of Irish folklore. However, they were hunted to extinction; the last reliable observation of a wolf in Ireland came from County Carlow when a wolf was hunted and killed near Mount Leinster in 1786 for killing sheep.

   The **red squirrel** has also been in Ireland since before the last ice age. It is now quite rare in Ireland due to the removal of native woodlands. It is absent from areas along the west and north coasts. Another factor leading to the decline of the red squirrel was the introduction in 1911 of the grey squirrel who competes with the red squirrel for food.

Fig. 3 Red squirrels were common in Ireland before forest clearance.

Fig. 4 Wolves were part of the cool temperate forest biome in Ireland until the eighteenth century.

- **Twentieth century (1900 – 2000):** By the early 1900s, only 0.5% (35,000 hectares) of the land area of Ireland was covered by woodland. Remnants of the great Irish forests survive in a few parkland areas such as Killarney National Park in County Kerry and Glenveigh National Park in County Donegal.

- **Today:** Roughly 12% of the land area of Ireland is under coniferous woodland: this is the lowest in Europe. The European Union average for woodland is 31%. It is hoped that we will have 16% of the land of Ireland under woodland by 2035. This will be a great achievement, but it still means Ireland will have just over half the EU average.

5.2 The impact of deforestation on the tropical rainforest biome

Felling of the tropical rainforest has a global and local impact. The destruction of large areas of the biome in many countries such as Brazil, Madagascar and Indonesia influences the global climate. In this section we will focus on deforestation in Brazil and the global impact of felling tropical rainforests.

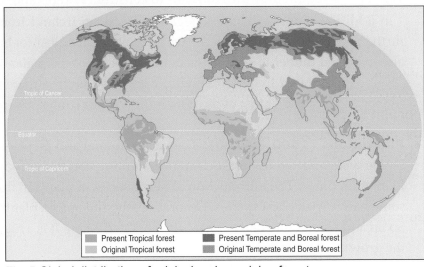

Fig. 5 Global distribution of original and remaining forests

Causes of deforestation in Brazil

In Brazil forests are under threat from the following human activities:

1. Intensive agriculture, which requires forest to be cleared to grow crops/grass, e.g. soya bean plantations and cattle ranching.
2. Logging companies cut down trees to sell their timber.
3. Construction of large dams and reservoirs that drown forest.
4. Mining and industry clear forest to reach minerals.
5. Government-sponsored forest colonisation schemes clear forest for road building, urbanisation and farming.

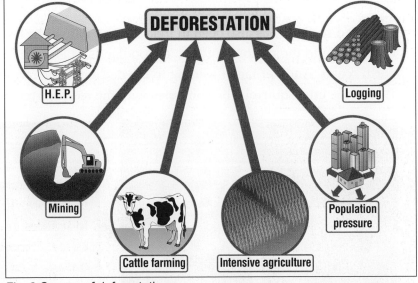

Fig. 6 Causes of deforestation

Worldwide, an area of rainforest the size of Belgium is felled each year.

74

The causes of deforestation are listed on page 74. However, the reason why this deforestation has been allowed to happen is due to **government policy** and the **social and economic development needs of Brazil**.

Government policy, agricultural and economic needs

(a) Government policy: During the 1950s and 1960s a new capital city, Brasilia, was built in the heart of the Amazon rainforest. This was to encourage the settlement of the region in order to exploit its economic resources. Today Brasilia has a population of 2.3 million people.

To construct the city, large areas of forest were cleared. More deforestation occurred on the outskirts of the city where small, temporary housing settlements were built for the migrant workers who moved to this area in order to construct the new capital city. Instead of returning to their original homes upon completion of the city, these workers chose to stay and avail of the greater opportunities in Brasilia.

In the 1970s and 1980s overpopulation and poverty in other Brazilian cities created political difficulties. In order to relieve the population pressure in these urban areas, the government began to encourage poor people from the cities to settle in the forest and clear it for farming. In some cases, land was given away. This actively promoted the further destruction of the forest.

Fig. 7 The construction of Brasilia led to deforestation.

(b) Agricultural development: In Brazil, modern forest settlers and developers can gain ownership of Amazonian lands by simply clearing forest and placing a few head of cattle on the land. Cattle are a low-risk investment relative to cash crops (soya, coffee) which are subject to wild price swings and pest infestations. Beef producers require more land to herd massive numbers of cattle for the beef trade with Europe and North America. This has led to uncontrolled forest burning to make new pasture.

Cash crop production is another important cause of deforestation. The need to repay international debt has led to the increase in the production of cash crops for export, e.g. soya bean.

The increase in deforestation due to soya bean farming has been so great that in response to international campaigns by environmental groups such as Greenpeace a ban or moratorium was established in 2006 by the Brazilian Association of Vegetable Oil Industries and the National Association of Cereal Exporters. This ban requires major traders to buy soya from areas deforested before June 2006 instead of soya grown on newly-cut forest. The moratorium is seen as a model for other commodities linked to deforestation, including cattle products, sugar cane and palm oil.

Fig. 8 Cattle ranch

Fig. 9 Uncontrolled forest burning

(c) Economic development: The Brazilian government continues to open up the Brazilian rainforest to take advantage of its timber and mineral wealth.

Timber companies are given rights to remove forest and sell timber abroad. The Brazilian government receives a portion of the timber companies' profits and uses it to pay off international debts. As the area is rich in resources, licences are given to mining companies to clear forests and mine for metals such as iron ore and copper.

Illegal growing and felling of timber is also leading to rapid deforestation, fuelled by a demand for cheap supplies of plywood and tropical timber locally and abroad. Illegal timber is estimated to account for 80% of all timber produced in the Brazilian Amazon.

Fig. 10 Mining is a cause of deforestation in Brazil.

(d) Transport development: Roads are being built across the Amazon rainforest to allow access to logging companies, mineral exploration companies, soya plantations, cattle ranches and hydroelectric power (HEP) stations. To construct these roads, large tracts of forest were cleared.

The longest road is the Trans-Amazonian Highway, a 5,300 km road, built across Brazil from east to west. This highway was designed to facilitate settlement and the exploration of resources in this vast under-populated river basin. It has allowed the movement of people and goods to previously inaccessible areas. In order to encourage people to move to the region, settlers are granted a 100-hectare plot of land, six-months' salary and easy access to agricultural loans. This is in exchange for settling along the highway and converting the surrounding rainforest into agricultural land.

Fig. 11 Construction of roads is a cause of deforestation of tropical forests.

(e) Energy supplies: Brazilian industry requires more power if it is to develop and maintain its industrial strength. An unlimited water supply and ideal river conditions has led to the development of many HEP stations across the Amazon region. Over 125 new HEP dams have been built in the Brazilian rainforest (see Fig. 12, page 77). Each dam and reservoir floods many thousands of hectares of forest. The most controversial dam has been a proposed dam on the Xingu River due to the size of the reservoir and the area to be flooded.

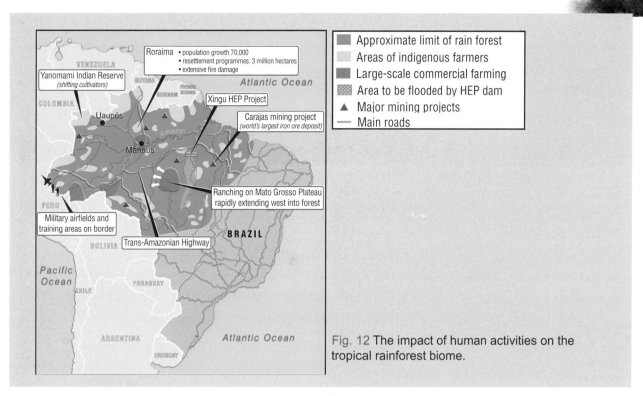

Fig. 12 The impact of human activities on the tropical rainforest biome.

The impact of deforestation on tropical rainforests

Rainforests have many uses. They prevent soil erosion, reduce the risk of floods, filter water, keep rivers healthy for fish and encourage pollination of plants by insects and birds. These functions are particularly important to the world's poorest people, who rely on natural resources for their everyday survival.

Globally, rainforests are disappearing at about 40 hectares per minute, day and night. This clearance is having a significant effect on the biome and its people.

Clearing the rainforest has several impacts on the biome and the world as Fig. 13 below shows.

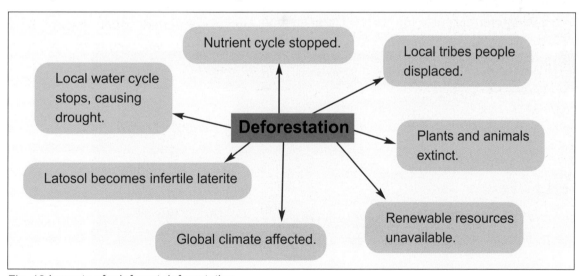

Fig. 13 Impacts of rainforest deforestation

1. Impact on people

- Deforestation has had a fatal impact on many tribal people. Before 1500, there were approximately six million native people living in Amazonia. By 2000, there were less than 250,000. By the twenty-first century, 90 tribes of native peoples had been wiped out in Brazil alone. In 2011 it was estimated that there were just over 100 un-contacted tribes around the world.

- Workers from the mining and logging companies and farm settlers spread diseases such as the common cold and measles. These diseases have killed hundreds of thousands of native Indians, as they have never been exposed to these germs before and therefore have no immunity to them.
- The area that was home to many native people is greatly reduced by deforestation. Their rights to land ownership have been ignored or neglected. Some tribal people may have been murdered for trying to resist the clearance of the rainforest by ranchers and forest companies in Brazil, Malaysia and Indonesia.
- The native rainforest people have also been denied access to the wealth generated by pharmaceutical companies who make drugs based on rainforest plants (see below) using tribal knowledge.
- Deforestation leads to a reduction of soil nutrients. Once the soil has become depleted of nutrients, it can no longer support the people who live there. The people are then forced to search for new lands to rebuild their farms and fields. As a result more deforestation occurs as these displaced farmers, peasants and ranchers fell more trees to maintain their way of making a living.

2. Impact on plants and animals

- The area of natural habitat for wildlife is severely reduced. Many animals and insects in the rainforest have not been clearly identified yet and as more of the rainforest is destroyed, the opportunity to study and identify these animals is lost.
- The loss of many species of plants is a serious cause for concern as some contain chemicals that could one day lead to cures for serious illnesses such as cancer and AIDS.
- We already get many common drugs from different species of tree, e.g. **aspirin**. About one quarter of all the medicines we use come from rainforest plants. **Curare** comes from a tropical vine and is used as an anaesthetic and to relax muscles during surgery. **Quinine**, from the cinchona tree, is used to treat malaria. More than 1,400 varieties of tropical plants are thought to contain potential cures for cancer. These are being lost, cut and burnt at an increasing rate.

Fig. 14 Clearance of tropical forests for agriculture in Bolivia. People have been settled in the forest to cultivate soya beans. Each agricultural pin-wheel pattern is centred on a small community. The communities are then spaced evenly across the landscape at 5-km intervals (central place theory). Roadways can be seen connecting each town centre.

3. Impact on soils

- When a forest is cleared, the nutrient cycle (Chapter 4, Fig. 5, page 55) is destroyed. The remaining latosol soil canbe easily washed away by heavy rain. In addition, as a result of the high temperatures in the tropical region, the exposed soil is baked into a hard, brick-like surface which cannot support plant growth. This is known as a **laterite** soil, which is useless for farming. Once the land has become depleted of nutrients, it can no longer support the inhabitants who then move to new lands. As a result, more deforestation occurs.

- Settlers who had been persuaded by the government to leave the cities and settle in these areas find that the land they had hoped to work is useless. Many move back to urban areas as a result adding to urban problems in developing countries, e.g. shanty towns.

Fig. 15 Beef cattle do not thrive on grassland grown on latosols

- The grass growth on the latosols is so poor that the beef cattle do not thrive and even more land is cleared to feed them or smaller animals are grazed. In mountainous areas such as Indonesia soil erosion occurs within days of forest clearance, reducing the productivity of the soil even more.

- Deforestation can reduce the amount of carbon that the soil can absorb from the atmosphere. Within ten years of deforestation the amount of carbon in the soil is reduced by more than half. This can contribute to global warming and also means the soil is less fertile.

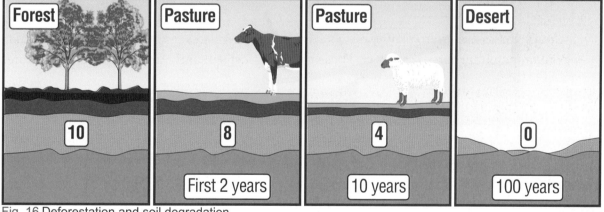

Fig. 16 Deforestation and soil degradation

Global impact of deforestation of the tropical rainforests

The rainforests regulate local and global weather through their absorption and formation of rainfall and their production/storage of atmospheric gases such as oxygen and CO_2. Felling the tropical rainforests has effects that are felt far beyond the local area.

Impact on global climate

- The loss of vast amounts of trees in the tropical rainforests is contributing to **global warming**. This is happening in two ways: first, the burning of forest adds CO_2 to the atmosphere. Second, by removing the forest we are destroying an important **carbon sink**. A carbon sink is a thing or place where carbon dioxide is taken from the air and stored for a period of time. Plants and animals act as carbon sinks as they take CO_2 into the cells of their bodies.

- As we have examined, deforestation reduces the amount of carbon held in soils. Once trees are removed, carbon that would have been locked into the soil now stays in the atmosphere.
- Deforestation affects **rainfall patterns**. In the water cycle, moisture is transpired by rainforest plants and evaporated into the atmosphere. This moisture forms rain clouds before being precipitated as rain back onto the forest. When the forests are cut down, less moisture is released into the atmosphere resulting in the formation of fewer rain clouds. Subsequently there is a decline in rainfall. The area then experiences drought. If rains stop falling, within a few years the area can become arid with the strong tropical sun baking down on the scrub-land. For example, Madagascar is today largely a red, treeless desert due to generations of deforestation.

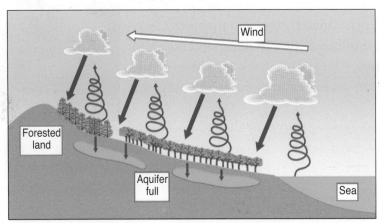

Fig. 17 Water cycle over forested land

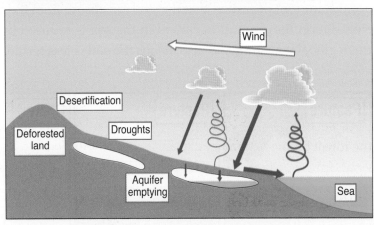

Fig. 18 Water cycle over deforested land

- Remaining forests are often at risk from **devastating fires** as has happened in Indonesia and Brazil.
- Deforestation changes the reflectivity (**albedo**) of the earth's surface. Over thick tropical vegetation, rising warm air takes moisture (provided by the same plant cover) up into the atmosphere, where it condenses to form clouds and rain. In this way tropical forests cool the planet by producing reflective clouds. These clouds increase the surface albedo and reflect the sun's energy back into space. (See Fig. 20, page 81.) Once an area is deforested the moisture is reduced and clouds do not form, the albedo is then reduced and more solar energy is absorbed by the atmosphere.

Fig. 19 Rainforests help to regulate the water cycle.

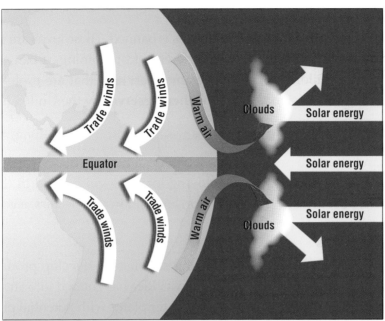

Fig. 20 Clouds produced by tropical forests reflect incoming solar energy.

Reducing the impact of deforestation

Rainforests are such an important resource that they will continue to be exploited in the future. The issue is how damage caused by this exploitation can be reduced. Several possible solutions to this issue exist.

1. Agri-forestry

- Agri-forestry involves combining farming and forestry. In the rainforest, farming has been carried out at the expense of forests. However, using agri-forestry, farms and forests can exist together in the future. People and wildlife benefit from this system. People can get an income from the forest while the forest biome is damaged as little as possible. See Fig. 21.
- Agri-forestry protects the forest surrounding the farms. It also reduces soil erosion and improves soil fertility by providing as much vegetation cover for the soil as possible. Agri-forestry also provides an income for native tribal people.

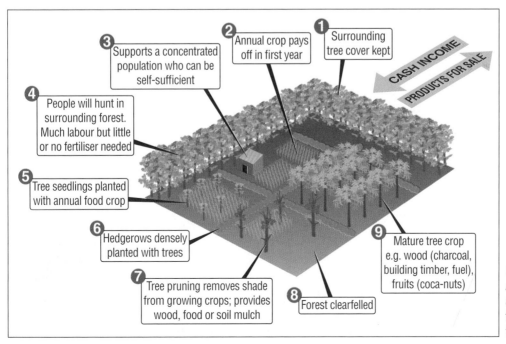

Fig. 21 Agri-forestry allows farms and forests to exist together

2. Conservation

Conservation zones are areas where felling of trees is banned. These areas are used only by native tribes and their way of life is secure from interference from mining, urban settlement, logging, HEP schemes and road building. Brazil has many forest sites that are protected. Some of these sites are so unique they are designated as **biosphere reserves** by the United Nations.

3. Ecotourism

Ecotourism can fund efforts to protect and rehabilitate degraded forests. Money from ecotourism is earned through park entrance fees, employing locals as guides and in the services (hotels, restaurants, drivers, boat drivers, porters, cooks) and handicrafts sectors, e.g. Costa Rica.

4. Bio–prospecting fees

Rainforest countries can earn money by allowing scientists to develop products from the plant and animal species in the forests. For example, Costa Rica has entered into an agreement with the American pharmaceutical company, Merck, to look for plants with potential pharmaceutical uses. Under the agreement, a portion of the proceeds from plant/animal products that do prove commercially valuable will go to the Costa Rican government which has guaranteed that some of the royalties will be set aside for conservation projects.

5.3   The impact of intensive agriculture on biomes

Intensive agriculture has already had and continues to have a major impact on biomes across the world. Intensive agriculture often occurs as a developing country tries to repay debts, deal with population growth and improve its economy.

> **Intensive agriculture** is a type of farming whereby large amounts of crops or animal products are produced from an area of land (high yields). In order to get such high yields from the land intensive farming uses large amounts of money, labour, artificial fertilisers, water and pesticides.

> **You must study one of the choices below:**
> The impact of intensive agriculture on the tropical rainforest biome OR
> The impact of intensive agriculture on the hot desert biome.

Choice 1:   The impact of intensive agriculture on the tropical rainforest biome

Intensive agriculture, especially the production of soya beans, has important effects on the tropical rainforest biome. Intensive agriculture completely disrupts the natural ecological balance of the rainforest in the following ways:

(a) Large-scale slash-and-burn of rainforest

(b) Addition of artificial fertilisers and illegal chemicals to river water

(c) Rainforest replaced by scrub vegetation and cash crop monoculture

(d) Pest infestations

(e) Disruption of water cycle and soil erosion

(a) Impact: Large-scale slash-and-burn

- In order to make a forest ready for farming, forest clearers use **slash-and-burn** techniques to clear land. Using this method forest is cut and then the area is burned. This releases nutrients locked up in the vegetation and produces a layer of nutrient-rich material above the infertile latosol soils of the tropical forest.

- Native tribes have always used this method of clearance but it has little impact on the forest because the area they clear is so small. In complete contrast intensive farming clears forests on a much larger scale. Instead of burning a small area (1-4 ha), intensive farmers slash and burn hundreds to thousands of hectares.

- The massive plantations used in intensive agriculture take up most of the fertile soils in the landscape. Therefore many smaller farmers have little choice but to move into and clear more forest for their own food and farmland.

Fig. 22 Burning rainforest

> For every quarter pounder hamburger consumed in the USA from rainforest-produced beef, about 5 m² of rainforest is cleared.

(b) Impact: Addition of artificial fertilisers and illegal chemicals to river water

- Once an area of forest is cleared, it is quickly planted and supports vigorous growth for a few years. Sixty to seventy per cent of land deforested in the Brazilian Amazon ends up as cattle pasture. Large numbers of cattle are grazed on the newly-cleared forest. At first each hectare of cleared land may support one animal, but after 3 years or so soil nutrients are so depleted that large amounts of expensive fertiliser are required to keep the farms in business. After 6-8 years, each animal may require five hectares.

- Fertiliser may be washed into local streams, affecting fish and aquatic life. Pesticides are also used to combat weeds in soya plantations. These chemicals wash or blow into other parts of the rainforest and pollute streams and rivers. They are harmful to plant and animal life alike.

- The illegal cultivation of coca plants (the active ingredient in cocaine) for the drugs trade is also polluting water in the rainforest biome in countries like Colombia. The most serious environmental concern (other than deforestation) is the illegal **dumping of chemicals** including kerosene, sulfuric acid and acetone which are used to process the coca leaves.

(c) Impact: Rainforest replaced by scrub vegetation and cash crop monoculture

- When the use of fertiliser is no longer economical, the land is abandoned and reverts to scrub vegetation. Drought-resistant grasses may move in or cattle ranchers may plant imported African grasses for cattle grazing. The land is now barely productive and only a small number of cattle can be grazed in the area.

- Where the land is suitable for agriculture, e.g. on river flood plains fed by fertile alluvium, large plantations of cash crops are cultivated in single crop plantations known as **monoculture**, e.g. rice, citrus fruits, oil palms, coffee, tea, soya beans, cocoa, rubber and bananas. The cash crop plantations are often highly mechanised and the heavy machinery can lead to soil

compaction and also soil erosion. Soya bean production increased dramatically once climate resistant varieties were developed.

- In 2010 more than 62 million tonnes of soya was produced on a land area in Brazil that was nearly the size of Britain. Animals and plants native to the rainforest biome cannot survive in the plantations and so the natural ecological balance that existed is disrupted or completely destroyed.

Fig. 23 Plantations in Brazil

(d) Impact: Pest infestations

- In natural rainforest, widespread pest infestations are rare because individuals of a given species are widely dispersed. However intensive farming in the tropical climate causes problems. Planting a single crop makes the crop highly vulnerable to disease and pests, as recent insect infestations have shown in Brazil and India. To avoid infestations, more chemical pesticides are used on the farmland destroying weeds and pests but also destroying native plants and insects.
- The planting of these monocultures can also be economically risky with price changes so common in international commodities markets. A single cold spell, pest attack or drought can devastate a huge part of the agricultural economy.

(e) Impact: Disruption of water cycle and soil erosion

The cultivation of crops in mountainous areas affects the water cycle and increases soil erosion. In Peru, the illegal cultivation of coca plants has been so widespread in the foothills of the Andes Mountains that annual river flood patterns have been changed. A lack of flooding leads to a loss of valuable alluvium. Soils then become infertile and more easily eroded when the rains fall. The water cycle is also disrupted by deforestation as you have already seen on page 80, in Figs 17 and 18.

Fig. 24 Deforestation for palm oil leads to more soil erosion in Madagascar. Note soil-choked river mouths.

Choice 2: The impact of intensive agriculture on the hot desert biome

Desert soils are rich in mineral nutrients but lack water due to the dry climate. Intensive agriculture is possible in the hot desert biome due to irrigation. Irrigation is the artificial application of water to soils in dry areas. Water for irrigation can come from wells, rivers, canals, lakes and reservoirs. Often dams are built to supply water for irrigation.

Fig. 25 Irrigation allows the growth of crops in desert areas beside the Dead Sea.

Irrigation has enabled desert soils in many countries such as Saudi Arabia, the USA (e.g. California), Israel and Egypt to be extremely productive.

Crops such as cotton, rice, cashew nuts, beans, olives, figs, peaches, citrus fruits, vegetables, cereals, sugar cane, apricots and pomegranates are grown in irrigated regions.

Groundwater is a major source of water in desert areas. Although the Sahara Desert is now the largest desert in the world, during the last ice age it was grassland with a climate similar to that of present-day Kenya and Tanzania. The annual rainfall was much greater than it is now, creating many rivers and lakes. The rains filled a series of vast underground **aquifers**. Since then the climate has changed and human activities have added to

Almost one third of the world population depends on groundwater for its water needs and more than 70% of these resources are used in the agriculture industry.

the natural desertification of the region. Modern African nations are now mining this **fossil water** to support irrigated farming projects. Fossil water is mined from depths of 1 km and pumped to the surface. However, it is not being replenished under current climatic conditions.

Fig. 26 Irrigation channel in desert area

Fig. 27 Central Pivot irrigation - each circle is a kilometre wide. Water is pumped from a central well and sprayed over the crops.

Fig. 28 Irrigation in Saudi Arabia

Fig. 29 Oasis in Morocco, Africa

Intensive agriculture has had an impact on desert regions mainly because of irrigation. The main impacts of intensive agriculture on the desert biome are:

(a) Damage to the soil due to increased salinity

(b) Pollution of ground water and oases

(c) Land subsidence

(d) Destruction of natural habitat

(a) Impact: Damage to soil due to increased salinity

Poorly-drained irrigated land leaves behind salt deposits as the water evaporates. The salt can be in many forms including sodium chloride, calcium, magnesium, carbonate, bicarbonate and sulfate. In many places, fields that once grew healthy crops of grains are now encrusted in salt. Crops fail and production is reduced. More than a quarter of the world's irrigated land has become so salty that many crops will no longer grow there.

Salt affects plants in the following ways:

* It can be directly toxic to plant tissue, e.g. leaf burn and defoliation.
* It can prevent the plant taking the nutrients it needs from the soil. For example, relatively high levels of calcium can inhibit the uptake of iron.
* It can cause the plants difficulty in extracting soil water they need for growth.
* To make the land productive again, the fields have to be flooded up to four times to clear away the salt.

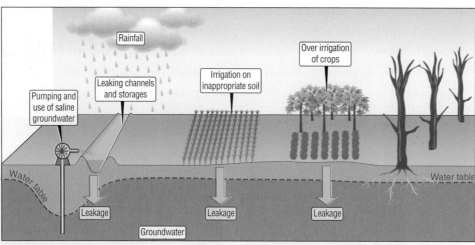

Fig. 30 Inappropriate irrigation can poison land through salinisation.

(b) Impact: Pollution of ground water and oases

Irrigation also causes large amounts of salts, fertilisers and pesticides to be flushed into rivers and streams that occur in desert regions. In the south-west USA, 37% of the salinity of the Colorado River is due to irrigation water flowing into it. The river carries an estimated nine million tonnes of salts annually. The concentration of salt in the water of the lower Colorado River valley is so high that it cannot be used for human consumption without treatment. When water is very scarce in developing countries such as Chad, untreated sewage water is often used to irrigate crops. This can lead to disease such as dysentery and cholera.

The environmental impacts from stream salinity include:

* Decline of native vegetation and loss of habitat.
* Loss of nesting sites and decline in bird populations

- Decline in wildlife fauna.
- Reduced food for wildlife populations.
- Increased soil and wind erosion.

(c) Impact: Land subsidence

- The drilling of wells for irrigation, farming and animal herding can trigger land subsidence in desert regions. These subsidences tend to occur in land where the ground contains thick deposits of fine sands, silt, and clays.
- Subsidence occurs because the amount of water drawn from the ground is greater than the amount of rain that falls. The constant extraction of ground water for irrigation causes the water table to drop. As water is pumped to the surface, the spaces of the pores in the soils and rock joints and bedding planes are emptied. This can cause subsidence as the ground settles down under its own weight.
- In southern and central Arizona water table levels have declined between 91 and 152 metres and the land has subsided 3.8 metres since the early 1940s. In the San Joaquin Valley of the United States, groundwater pumping for crops has gone on for generations. This has resulted in some areas of the valley floor sinking by over 30 metres.

(d) Impact: Destruction of natural habitat

- The natural vegetation in desert regions is also affected by intensive cattle grazing. In developing countries increasing numbers of cattle are affecting the desert biome around water holes.
  Domesticated herds move slowly and do not stray great distances from waterholes. They cause stress on pasture land around watering places, while the areas further away remain almost undisturbed.
  The result is increasingly degraded vegetation close to the waterhole.
    Around the waterhole itself, where the animals remain the longest, there is no vegetation at all, and the soil is over-fertilised by animal excrement.

Fig. 31 Collecting water at a new borehole in southern Ethiopia

- The destruction of plant cover usually leads to the formation of sand dunes in the areas of sandy soils. The normal vegetation cover may be found only at a great distance from the wells.
- In the south-west USA cattle grazing and sheep farming were introduced during the gold rush years of the nineteenth century. This grazing destroyed the natural desert vegetation and led to the growth of invasive weeds such as the tumbleweed.

Fig. 32 Desert tumbleweed

- Grazing can exert both positive and negative effects on desert vegetation. Positive effects include: a slight loosening of the soil surface; promotion of seed-setting by plants and pressing of seeds into the soil by hooves; and fertilisation of the soil through excrement. In contrast, with overgrazing, the soil is loosened too much and is blown away.

5.4 The impact of industrial activity on biomes

The impact of acid rain on the European coniferous forest biome

What is acid rain?

Acid rain refers to all types of precipitation such as rain, snow, sleet, hail and fog that has a pH less than 5.6.

Acid rain kills or damages trees, aquatic life, crops, other vegetation, buildings and monuments. It corrodes copper and lead piping, reduces soil fertility and can cause toxic metals to leach into underground drinking water sources.

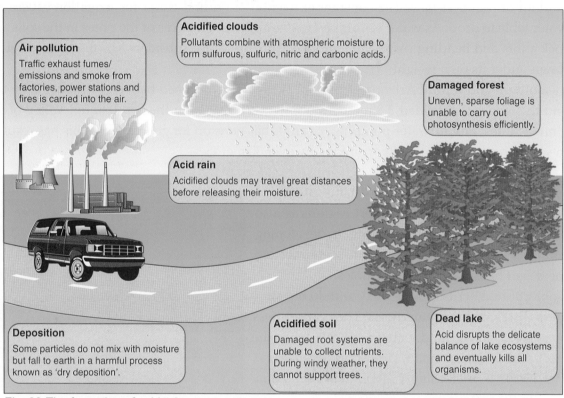

Fig. 33 The formation of acid rain

Two types of air pollutants – **sulfur dioxide** (SO_2) and **nitrogen oxides** (NO_x) – cause acid rain. These two gases are produced by power stations, factories and vehicles burning fossil fuels.

When these pollutants reach the atmosphere they combine with water in clouds and change to sulfuric acid and nitric acid. Winds may spread these acidic solutions across the atmosphere and over hundreds of kilometres. Rain, sleet, hail and

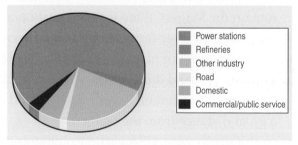

Fig. 34 Sources of sulfur dioxide emissions

snow wash these acids from the air onto the land. Some acid particles do not dissolve in the rain but fall as acidic dust called **dry deposition**.

Acidity is measured using a scale called the **pH scale**. This scale goes from 0 to 14. 0 is the most acidic and 14 is the most alkaline (opposite of acidic). Something with a pH value of 7 is neutral. This means that it is neither acidic nor alkaline. Very strong acids will burn if they touch your skin and can even destroy metals. Acid rain is much, much weaker than this; it is never acidic enough to burn your skin. Vinegar has a pH value of 2.2 and lemon juice has a value of pH of 2.3. Even the strongest recorded acid rain is only about as acidic as lemon juice or vinegar, but it is very damaging when it falls as acid rain.

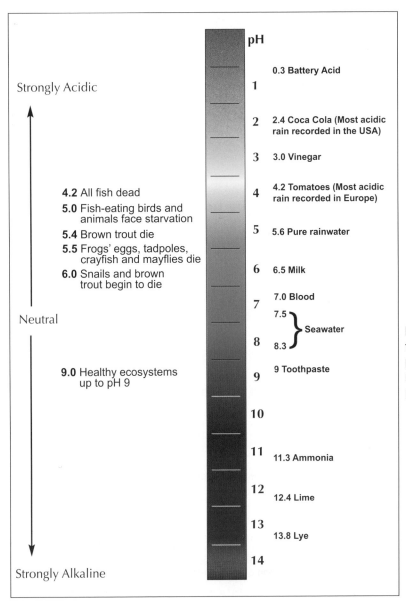

Strongly Acidic

4.2 All fish dead
5.0 Fish-eating birds and animals face starvation
5.4 Brown trout die
5.5 Frogs' eggs, tadpoles, crayfish and mayflies die
6.0 Snails and brown trout begin to die

Neutral

9.0 Healthy ecosystems up to pH 9

Strongly Alkaline

pH

1
2
3
4
5
6
7
8
9
10
11
12
13
14

0.3 Battery Acid
2.4 Coca Cola (Most acidic rain recorded in the USA)
3.0 Vinegar
4.2 Tomatoes (Most acidic rain recorded in Europe)
5.6 Pure rainwater
6.5 Milk
7.0 Blood
7.5 } Seawater
8.3 }
9 Toothpaste
11.3 Ammonia
12.4 Lime
13.8 Lye

Fig. 35 The pH scale goes from 0 to 14. Acids have a pH of from 0 to 6, 7 is neutral and bases have a pH of from 8 to 14.

Acid rain is a particular concern for coniferous forests in Scandinavia and Eastern Europe. It is estimated that more than 65% of trees in the UK and over 50% of trees in Germany, the Netherlands and Switzerland are affected by die-back due to acid rain. (Die-back is the gradual dying of plant shoots, beginning at their tips, due to climatic conditions – such as acid rain – or various diseases.)

Nature is tolerant of some acidic deposition. The soils and water can absorb some levels of acidity in the air without harmful effects on plants, water and animals. However, above a certain **critical load,** damage to the environment occurs. For example, in European forests the critical load for sulfur in the air is 10-20 micrograms per cubic metre of air. Above this level, forests are damaged. Lichens are most sensitive to acid rain. They begin to die at levels of 10 micrograms of sulfur per cubic metre of air. Critical levels are exceeded in many areas of Europe and risk of damage is widespread as Fig. 36 shows.

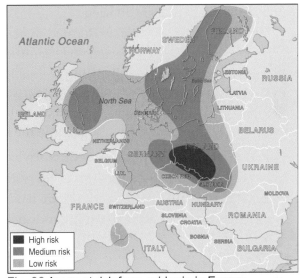

High risk
Medium risk
Low risk

Fig. 36 Areas at risk from acid rain in Europe

The effects of acid rain on European forests

Acid rain has a variety of effects on the European coniferous forest biome.

(a) Impact: Nutrient leaching of soils

- Some of the most important effects of acid rain on forests involve nutrient leaching. Nutrient leaching occurs when acid rain displaces calcium, magnesium and potassium from soil particles, depriving trees of these important plant minerals. The soils which are most easily damaged by acid rain are those whose parent rock is acidic, e.g. sandstone or granite.

(b) Impact: Poisoning and damage of plants by toxic metals

- Toxic metals such as lead, zinc, copper, chromium and aluminium produced by industrial activity are deposited in the forest from the atmosphere. Acid rain then releases these metals into the soils. The metals stunt the growth of trees, mosses, algae, nitrogen-fixing bacteria and fungi needed for forest growth.
- Acid rain further damages plants in the following ways: The waxy surface of leaves is broken down and nutrients are lost, making trees more susceptible to frost, fungi and insects. Root growth slows and as a result fewer nutrients are taken up. The trees essentially starve to death.

(c) Impact: Release of aluminium into rivers and lakes

- It is in aquatic habitats that the effects of acid rain are most obvious. Acid rain runs off the land and ends up in streams, lakes and marshes – the acid rain also falls directly on these areas.
- When the pH of water is below 5.5, fish die or become seriously ill. Acid rain makes waters acidic and causes them to absorb the aluminum that makes its way from soil into lakes and streams. This combination makes waters toxic to crayfish, clams, fish and other aquatic animals.
- As the acidity of a lake increases, the water becomes clearer and the numbers of fish and other water animals decline. Freshwater shrimps, snails and mussels are the most quickly affected by acidification followed by fish such as minnows, salmon and roach. The eggs and young of the fish are the worst affected. The acidity of the water can cause deformity in young fish and can prevent eggs from hatching properly. Fish struggle to take in oxygen because their gills are affected.
- Some 14,000 Swedish lakes, located in acidic crystalline rocks, have been affected by acidificatio causing widespread damage to plant and animal life.
- Lakes and rivers can have powdered limestone added to them to neutralise the water – this is called **liming**. Liming, however, is expensive and its effects are only temporary. The governments of Norway and Sweden have successfully used liming to help restore dead lakes and streams in their countries but it is a continuing process as acid rain is still being produced by industrial activity.

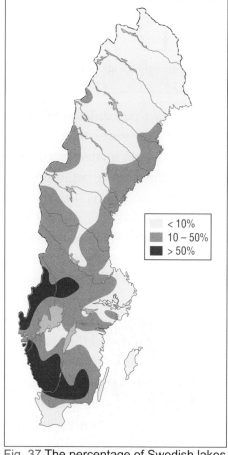

Fig. 37 The percentage of Swedish lakes affected by acidification

Chapter Revision Questions

1. Name three human activities that can change biomes.

2. Briefly outline how the spread of historic settlement led to the clearance of the deciduous forest biome in Ireland.

3. Name three causes of deforestation in Brazil.

4. Explain how these three causes resulted in deforestation in Brazil.

5. Name and explain three global problems caused by destruction of tropical rainforests.

6. What effect has intensive agriculture had on the tropical rainforest biome?

7. Describe the impact of rainforest clearance on people, wildlife and soils.

8. Describe the impact of intensive agriculture on the desert biome.

9. (a) What is acid rain?
   (b) Explain how acid rain is formed.
   (c) Draw a labelled diagram to show the formation of acid rain.

10. What is the effect of acid rain on the coniferous forest biome of Europe?

11. Look at the table below: With reference to the table, describe the trends shown.

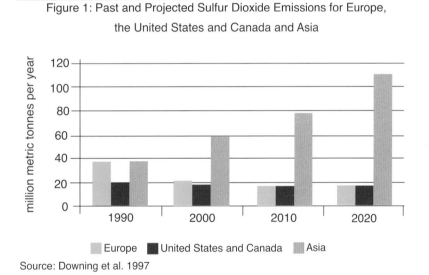

SO$_2$ Emissions in Asia Could Triple

Figure 1: Past and Projected Sulfur Dioxide Emissions for Europe, the United States and Canada and Asia

Source: Downing et al. 1997

12. Look at the diagram showing the pathways that acid rain might take. Explain what is happening at positions A to G.

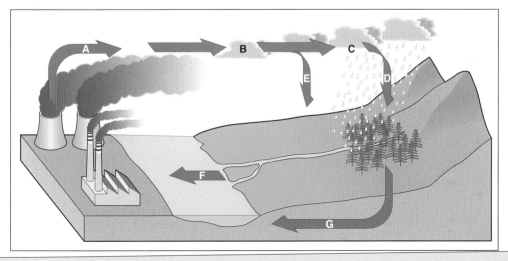

Exam Questions

13. Assess the impact of human activity on a biome that you have studied.

[80 marks]

LC Exam Paper

14. Assess the global implications of the continued felling of tropical rainforests.

[80 marks]

LC Sample Paper

15. 'A combination of factors is leading to the rapid loss of forest in Brazil.'
Discuss this statement in detail.

[80 marks]

16. 'Economic development has an impact on biomes.'
Discuss this statement with reference to a biome that you have studied.

[80 marks]

17. Assess how biomes have been altered by human activity.

[80 marks]

LC Exam Paper

18. Examine two ways in which human activities have altered the natural characteristics of a biome that you have studied.

[80 marks]

LC Exam Paper

Index

Answer Plan Chart: Option 7

You may choose 3 or 4 aspects of discussion for each answer.
See completed sample chart on next page. It is expected that you would expand on the points contained in each box in your answer.

Question	Aspect 1	Aspect 2	Aspect 3	Aspect 4
SRP 1				
2				
3				
4				
5				
6				
7				
8				

Question **2010 Q16** What influence does climate have on the characteristics of a Biome?	Aspect 1 **Characteristic:** Soil type	Aspect 2 **Characteristic:** Vegetation	Aspect 3 **Characteristic:** Animals
SRP 1	Climate influences the rainfall/water content	Climate influences the type of vegetation, e.g. cactus/mahogany tree	Climate influences the type of animal via adaptation to the vegetation, e.g. tree living or burrowing
SRP 2	Climate influences the soil-forming processes/ laterisation/ calcification/salinisation	Climate influences the rate of growth	Climate influences animal adaptation to plant food supply.
SRP 3	Climate influences humus content via short nutrient cycle	Climate influences adaptations to water storage/water shedding	Climate influences animal lifestyle (arboreal/ground dwelling/nocturnal)
SRP 4	Climate determines soil colour (via humus content)	Climate influences structure of plants, e.g. buttress roots, tap roots	Climate influences animal/plant relationships, e.g. flying squirrel
SRP 5	Climate makes soil zonal	Climate influences plant relationships, e.g. epiphytes/lianas	Climate influences animal camouflage techniques, e.g. leaf-shaped/pale brown
SRP 6	Climate determines texture (via type of weathering)	Climate influences animal/plant relationships, e.g. hummingbird	Climate influences biodiversity in biome
SRP 7	Climate determines depth of soil	Climate influences growing season length/diurnal temperature range	Example should be given in all aspects for SRPs, e.g. tropical rainforest/desert
SRP 8	Climate determines structure (via type of weathering).	Climate influences method of plant reproduction, e.g. all year or ephemeral	Note: Marking Scheme did not accept 'climate' as an 'aspect' of discussion.